BEFORE YOU GO

General Editor

EMILY BENNETT

BEFORE YOU GO

Wisdom from
10 Women
WHO SERVED INTERNATIONALLY

B&H
PUBLISHING
BRENTWOOD, TENNESSEE

Published by B&H Publishing Group
Brentwood, Tennessee

Dewey Decimal Classification: 266.073
Subject Heading: WOMEN MISSIONARIES / MISSIONS /
WOMEN

Cover design by B&H Publishing Group.
Illustration by ilyakalinin/vectorstock.
Author photo by Erin Krizo.

1 2 3 4 5 6 • 27 26 25 24 23

To: Anabelle

May these women and others like them be examples
you look to as you follow Jesus—whatever the cost.

Acknowledgments

MY GRATEFULNESS TO the nine women who have contributed to this book cannot be adequately expressed in words. Thank you for being willing to be a part of this project. Thank you for baring a bit of your soul in hopes that it can encourage women as they seek to follow the Lord. Many of you have been friends and mentors to me. I admire each of you.

Thank you to B&H and Mary Wiley for allowing this idea to come to fruition. Thank you for caring deeply about equipping women for missions. Honestly, I never in a million years thought you would say yes to this idea. The risk you took to take on this project means the world to me.

Thank you to my mom and dad, who faithfully said hard goodbyes, spent holidays without kids and grandkids, took numerous trips to visit, and allowed us to live in your home too many times to count. Thank you for being an example of people who believe the gospel and who sent well even when it was at great personal cost.

Thank you to the two churches that have had profound impacts on my walk with God. To the Summit Church in North Carolina: thank you for teaching me that Jesus is better than anything this world could give or take away. You sent us well. Thank you to Grace Baptist Church in Cedarville, Ohio, for teaching me what it means to love the local church up close. Thank you for receiving us back well.

Thank you to my husband Matt. You are the best human I know. Thank you for believing in this project more than I did most of the time. Thank you for caring and valuing women's work in missions deeply. You push me both to think clearly about missions and ministry while not losing the love for the God who is at work in the world.

Thank you for listening to me reread the same sentence over and over again and never being annoyed—or maybe you were annoyed, but never showed it. I love you.

Contents

Introduction

Emily Bennett

I REMEMBER READING Elisabeth Elliot's *Through Gates of Splendor* while in grad school. She was my hero, a faithful woman to whom God had entrusted much. Elisabeth suffered and endured trial after trial. She had so much wisdom to give. I knew the story of Amy Carmichael and the incredible call God put on her life, and I had read of the Lord's faithfulness to her through more than fifty-five years of missionary work in India without a break. I had read of Lottie Moon, the firecracker of a saint who endured much in China, leading both women and men to come to know the Lord. Through their biographies and words, these women showed me the faithfulness of God, encouraged me to take risks for the gospel, and helped me understand that suffering is a normal part of the Christian journey. For that, I am forever grateful.

I, however, found myself at the beginning of my own missionary journey. I knew without a shadow of a doubt that God was calling my husband and me to overseas missions. Yet, when I read the wise words of these giants of the faith who had gone before me, I was intimidated. They had all my respect and admiration. I had learned so much from their lives.

But I was not them.

I loved God and I wanted to serve Him. All the paths our lives had taken had clearly led us to the point of packing our bags and leaving for worlds unknown. Still, I felt like there was no way I could live up to the women who had gone before me. Along with these great heroes of the faith, I wanted and needed the voices of those I considered "ordinary" to speak into my life, women like me who had heard the call to go and who simply went out of a love for God and a desire to be obedient. I wanted the wisdom of women who had gone before me, cherishing God's kingdom more than their own comfort, to speak into my life. I wanted their victories and mistakes to guide me. I wanted them to mentor me, even if it was merely mediated through their ink spilled on a page.

This book is born out of that desire. I hope that through these pages you will hear the relatable voices of everyday saints cheering you on as you prepare for and encounter your first years on the mission field. I could not write it on my own. I needed the collective wisdom of other women whom I love and admire to pour into you *before you go*. I want these stories to be a companion to you when you are lonely and wisdom when you need guidance. I want these testimonies to solidify your obedience to follow the Lord wherever He would take you, whether bravely going alone as a single woman or bravely taking your kids someplace dangerous. Frankly, I want these words to speak courage into the fearful yes that you have offered the Lord in response to whatever assignment He would give you. This book is for you, ladies, *before you go*.

A BIT OF BACKGROUND

My husband and I landed in the Middle East in early 2011. We had been rerouted to a different country than we had planned because the Arab Spring had just erupted a month before we left. After being picked up and dropped off at our new home, we sat jet-lagged on our stained yellow couch with trunks all around us. We had made it. We sat in the middle of the Middle East in the dead of winter, alone. I remember thinking, *What now?* It took so much to get here; what happens once we arrive? We left with fanfare, a massive commissioning ceremony, and our church cheering us on. But when we landed, we found ourselves in a cold, dark, dirty house confronted with the overwhelming task of making disciples among people who really didn't care that we had arrived.

We had no idea how difficult and incredible the years to come would be, and how we would come to know the goodness of God when life fell apart. We had no idea how beautiful it would be to watch someone read Scripture and understand Jesus to be their Savior for the very first time. We had no idea how much endurance it would take to get up and do the same thing over and over again—only to be rejected over and over again. Though we had been told ahead of time that team was a big deal, we had no idea how key of a role team would play in our day-to-day lives. As a married woman, I had not foreseen what an integral role our single teammates would play within the life of our team and family. I had not anticipated the variety of views on how married women should function on the field, nor how those views affected ministry on the ground. I had no idea how living and working overseas would lay me flat on my face in utter dependence on the Lord. I had no idea how incredibly sweet it would be to know our Savior more intimately as a result of living in a place that was difficult to consider "home." I discovered so many things that I did not know.

This book exists as an attempt to share with you some of the things we have learned along the way to give you a head start on your own journey. I want you to hear about God's faithfulness to women who said yes because they knew the Lord, not necessarily because they knew what they were doing. Though I would love to tell you how extraordinary these women are, honestly, they are pretty normal. Some of them spent careers on the field. Some of them spent a handful of years overseas before God called them back. We all come from different places, and we all ministered in different contexts. Some of us went overseas excited and eager to go. Others of us went internally kicking and screaming. Our stories are all different. But I want you, reader, to have a collection of our experiences in your hands as our encouragement and advice to you as you begin. I believe that these pages are littered with hard-earned wisdom that has been forged in the fire of adversity, mistakes, failure, and faith. I pray that it is a blessing to your soul as you see sisters who have walked this road ahead of you. And I pray more than anything that you see the faithfulness of our God who is willing to use us all—cracked vessels that we are—to display His glory among the nations.

So this book is for you, ordinary girl, taking the step of faith—maybe alone, maybe with your family—to pack up and move overseas to proclaim the goodness of God to women in desperate need of this good news. The following chapters are a collection of thoughts that we want you to have *before you go.*

CHAPTER 1

Discerning Our Calling

Cyndi Logsdon

From the General Editor

CYNDI LOGSDON WAS a name that I had heard for several years, always in the context of the most glowing enthusiasm. I was told by my friends who were on her team what a good leader she was. I was told by people who knew her how sharp of a mind she had, and anyone I met who talked about her always complimented her kind spirit and encouraging disposition.

It was no surprise, then, that when my husband and I got to spend time with Cyndi and her husband, Scott, we found ourselves admiring them and their ministry. We spent several days with them in a small group during a missions training event in Europe, and both Matt and I commented that we wished we could work on their team.

As with the other ladies in this book, I selfishly wish that we had more time to sit together, and I wish our paths crossed more often in life and ministry. However, I am grateful she has taken the time to lend her voice to an aspect of missions that desperately needs to be central in our thinking. Cyndi and Scott have served throughout their ministry from a place of conviction that the church is central to missions. I hope that this chapter encourages you, dear sister, to treasure the Holy Spirit, the Word, and the church as you discern your call to missions. I pray that it will lead you to invest in your local church and to be invested in by it as you prepare to be sent and to go.

DISCERNING OUR CALLING

I'll never forget our stress and confusion as my husband, Scott, and I walked through the brightly colored booths that were scattered throughout the large room at a conference for missionary candidates. Tables were covered with scarves, miniature flags, and pictures of people from all around the world. Total information overload.

We attended this conference because we were trying to determine where we should serve overseas. A white-haired missionary from Africa played a video of his teammates traveling by canoe to the mud-floored hut where they lived, and we wondered: "Are we the right fit for ministry by canoe?" We prayerfully considered bustling cities in Europe where missionaries drank tea from porcelain cups with saucers. A team from the Middle East said that if we joined their work we'd live on a compound, and I imagined seeing the world through the veil of a burka.

We were willing to go anywhere, but we needed discernment and we longed to hear God tell us what He wanted us to do.

> Now in the church at Antioch there were proph-
> ets and teachers: Barnabas, Simeon who was
> called Niger, Lucius of Cyrene, Manaen, a close
> friend of Herod the tetrarch, and Saul.
>
> As they were worshiping the Lord and
> fasting, the Holy Spirit said, "Set apart for me
> Barnabas and Saul for the work to which I have
> called them." Then after they had fasted, prayed,
> and laid hands on them, they sent them off.
> (Acts 13:1–3)

While the church in Antioch was worshiping and fasting, the Holy Spirit spoke. He told those gathered to set apart Barnabas and Saul for the work to which He had called them. Can you imagine what that was like? I have heard sermons reminding us that we don't know exactly what it means when God's Word says that the Holy Spirit spoke. Did everyone in the church at Antioch hear an audible voice and understand the word of the Lord at the same time? Did the church even realize at the time that He had spoken? We don't know the details, but we do know that Luke wrote the book of Acts under the inspiration of the Holy Spirit Himself. Therefore, if the Scripture says that He spoke, then rest assured, He spoke.

Saul and Barnabas were set apart by the Holy Spirit for the work to which they were called. At least in this one instance, we see that God called Saul and Barnabas in a corporate setting to do a specific work. "Calling" is a biblical concept. At the same time, calling may be one of the most misused and misunderstood terms Christians use when we talk about mission. When we use the term *calling* as God uses it, we are helped to learn more about God and about ourselves. However, when we use the term differently than authors of Scripture, we might be perpetuating misunderstanding and confusion.

I remember the day when a wonderful couple joined the work in Central Asia where we were serving. They were excited that God had "called" them to serve as church planters in this part of the world. Not long after they committed to join the team, we read their autobiographical sketch where they explained that they felt God had specifically called them to serve in a different region of the world—not Central Asia. When asked about what they had written, they said, yes, God had called them to serve in that other location, then a door was shut, and now God had called them to serve in Central Asia. Only a couple of months after they arrived, we heard that they had purchased tickets back to America and were returning home to their family. They told us that God had called them back home. They informed their direct supervisor of their decision and shared that they were called by God to return to the States. As you might expect, after some time in America, they contacted us and said God was now calling them back to Central Asia. We responded gently, but said, "We do not believe He is calling you back to our team at this time."

How could we turn them down when they believed they were called by God to join our team? We had been praying for the Lord of the harvest to send urgently needed laborers into the field. Shouldn't we warmly welcome this family to rejoin what God was doing among us?

As Christians, we take our calling seriously because God takes it seriously. The language of "calling" is used throughout

Scripture, so we need to understand how the Bible describes and defines this term. We take it seriously because we have been given a specific command to "make disciples of all nations" (Matt. 28:19) and we need to understand the part we are to play in that command. There's an urgency to take the gospel to those who have not yet heard. There are currently more than three billion people in the world today with little to no access to the gospel. That means that many people live their entire lives without ever even hearing the name of Jesus. So, how do we discern our specific role in this mission?

WHAT IS OUR CALLING?

To understand biblical calling, we must first agree that the Word of God is our ultimate authority and guide. If that is true, then we can have complete confidence when we read God's Word that we have heard the voice of God. We have actually heard God speak! We must also agree that the Bible is our only sure guide. The Bible tells us to seek godly counsel (Ps. 1:1) and pray for guidance (James 1:5)—but we must do these things in accordance with God's Word. We judge and discern the soundness of what we hear and believe by God's authoritative Word.

Therefore, what does the Bible tell us about our calling? The New Testament often uses the word *calling* to describe God's work of bringing us to salvation.[1] If we are in Christ, then we have been called to salvation (Matt. 9:13; Rom. 1:6; 8:30; Gal. 1:6; 1 Pet. 1:15–16). We also see in Scripture that a call to salvation always includes a call to mission (Matt. 28:19–20; Acts 1:8).[2] The Bible teaches that all who are in Christ are called, in some way, to make disciples of all nations.

After Jesus died, was buried, and rose again, He lived on earth for forty days and gave His disciples a mandate for how they were to spend the rest of their lives. This mandate is described in what we sometimes call the Great Commission passages of Scripture; the most familiar is Matthew 28:18–20. Jesus gave His final charge and commissioned His disciples to make disciples of all nations. David Platt reminds us, "The Great Commission is not just a general command to make disciples among as many people as possible. It is a specific command to make disciples among every people group in the world."[3] This is what the disciples were to spend their lives doing, and this is what we are to spend our lives doing as well. All followers of Jesus have been called to both salvation and to mission. These truths are clearly stated in God's authoritative Word, and we can build our lives upon them.

Yet often the specific details of how we are to be individually involved in mission aren't provided in Scripture. How do we know if God is calling us to be senders of missionaries like the church in Antioch? Or how do we know if God is calling us, like He called Saul and Barnabas, to be the ones who are sent by our local church? How do we choose a particular place of service when we are presented with so much need all around the world?

HOW DO WE DETERMINE GOD'S SPECIFIC WILL FOR OUR FUTURE?

This is the question we frequently ask when faced with important decisions; yet, this may be the wrong question. Christians sometimes think that to be obedient to God we need to first determine God's plan for our future. Once that is determined, then we are to be obedient to that revealed future direction in our lives. We just don't see that modeled in the Bible.

It may be helpful to first acknowledge that God is limitless, but we are not. There are limits to our knowledge and limits to what He has revealed to us even about His will. Deuteronomy 29:29 tells us, "The hidden things belong to the LORD our God, but the revealed things belong to us and our children forever, so that we may follow all the words of this law." Some things are hidden; yet, the revealed things of God belong to us. So, let's first consider what has been revealed.

There are events and circumstances that, in His sovereignty, God decrees. What God decrees will come to pass and cannot be thwarted. Some call this God's "decretive will." God has decreed that Jesus will return someday. This cannot change; it must and will happen. Some of God's decrees have been revealed, and we should plan our lives accordingly.

There are behaviors and circumstances that, in His sovereignty, God desires. Some call this His "preceptive" will, referring to His precepts, commandments, and laws.[4] God desires that His followers love one another as He has loved us (John 13:34). We may not always obey God's command, but Scripture is clear that He desires that we love one another.

Yet, there may be parts of God's will for us that have not been revealed. For example, we may need to choose a location on the mission field where we can serve. How do we choose between Africa and Asia when both are seemingly locations where God desires to send missionaries? We need to learn to make wise decisions as we seek to live a life of obedience in accordance with what God's Word tells us that He desires.

So, what question should we be asking? Maybe a question we should be asking is: "What are the usual means through which God speaks to His people to help them make wise decisions without knowing the full picture of the future?" Whether you have a flight booked and a date circled on your calendar when you will launch into a new culture to share the gospel or you are struggling through if God is calling you to go, this question guides every decision we make as Christians.

God Speaks to Us by His Son

> Long ago God spoke to our ancestors by the
> prophets at different times and in different ways.
> In these last days, he has spoken to us by his Son.
> (Heb. 1:1–2a)

First, God speaks to us through the Spirit of Christ living in us, so we must make decisions based on our union with Christ. We can study Jesus's life and see that not only in word, but also in deed, His entire life was focused on carrying out His Father's mission for Him and for the world. We can see that "the Son of Man [had] no place to lay his head" (Luke 9:58). He lived a transient life, going from town to town, teaching, healing, and calling the most unlikely people to a new kingdom and commissioning them to ministry (Matt. 4:18–25).

As we learn more about Jesus Himself, the knowledge that we are in Christ informs our life and actions (Heb. 1). Have you really thought about that before? If we are in Christ, and Christ is in us, we need to be about the work that He is currently completing in the world. Our Savior's last words on earth were a command to "go . . . and make disciples of all nations" (Matt. 28:19a). As we study various passages about Christ after His resurrection (Matt. 28:18–20; Luke 24:44–48; Acts 1:8; Matt. 16:18; Rev. 7:9), we see that Jesus is at work directing the proclamation and spread of the gospel and building His church. And He is doing all of that this very day through His people. Even after His ascension He didn't say to Saul, "Why are you persecuting my people?" Jesus said, "Saul, Saul, why are you persecuting *me*?" (Acts 9:4, emphasis mine), and then He gave Saul clear marching orders, and Saul was used by Jesus to build His church. If we are in Christ, and no longer live apart from Christ (Gal. 2:20), then our lives must be in alignment with what Christ was sent to accomplish: the proclamation of His glory among all nations (Luke 24:44–48).

God Speaks to Us through His Word

Second, God speaks to us through His Word. We can learn what God desires when we meditate on His Word. Second Timothy 3:16–17 reminds we have all we need to be complete and equipped for every good work God has prepared for us because of the inspired Word of God. This means that we make our life decisions based on how we can best obey God's clear commands. When we don't know what to do next, we strive to align our lives with what God's Word tells us that He desires for our lives.

Truth be told, when I have faced life-changing decisions, I have often hoped that God would send some clear sign in the sky to ensure that I am taking the right path. However, even without such signs, I can take comfort in the fact that James 1:5 promises wisdom for those who ask. As I meditate on Scripture and strive to align my life with God's commands, I can trust that the same God who ordered the steps of every disciple in history is also ordering my steps as I seek out His will. To this point, John Piper notes:

> [W]hen Paul told the Romans about his "ambition to preach the gospel, not where Christ has already been named," he never mentioned his dramatic experience. Instead, he quoted a verse of Scripture—Isaiah 52:15! "As it is written, 'Those who have never been told of him will see, and those who have never heard will understand'" (Rom. 15:20–22[ESV]).
>
> Why? Evidently, Paul's *personal* calling (not everyone is called to preach where Christ is not named) was confirmed and clarified by his meditation on Scripture.[5]

Remember that Paul did have a dramatic experience on the road to Damascus. Yet, it seems that his specific calling was clarified through meditation upon God's Word. God's Word may not specifically tell us whether we should serve in Africa or Asia, but it will guide and direct us (Ps. 119:105), and our job is to meditate on His Word, be obedient to His commands, and trust that He will care for us in the specific details of how our future unfolds—one step at a time.

God Speaks to Us as We Pray and Fast

Third, we seek the leading of the Holy Spirit through prayer and fasting. We are told that if we seek wisdom, God will grant

DISCERNING OUR CALLING

it generously (James 1:5). We seek wisdom because we are not the ones who determine the future. Our responsibility is to pursue God's preceptive will and use wisdom to guide us and help us discern. We know that if we call upon the Lord, He will answer us (Ps. 17:6). If we trust in the Lord and acknowledge Him in all our ways, He will direct our paths (Prov. 3:5–6). In Acts 13, when the Holy Spirit spoke to the church in Antioch, He spoke to them *while they were worshiping and fasting.*

God Speaks to Us through His Church

Fourth, God speaks to us through His church. When we are reconciled to Christ upon salvation, we are reconciled to His people (Eph. 2). Because of our union with Christ, we have supernatural communion with God's people. He has given us His church! Church leaders and church members are a gift to equip us for life and ministry (Eph. 4:11). The church helps us discern and make wise decisions. Through counsel from our church, we can see more clearly what our next steps should be as we follow Christ by obeying His precepts.

In Scripture, when we see specific instances of God calling people to a specific work, it's often in the context of God revealing His will *corporately* to the church. Look back at Acts 13. God told the church to set apart Saul and Barnabas (v. 2). He could have spoken to Saul as He had previously spoken to him on the road to Damascus when Saul was given a more general call. But even on the road to Damascus, when God spoke to Saul, others were involved. Saul was traveling with a group when he had this experience and God involved Ananias and others in the story. Likewise,

15

when God called Saul to begin his missionary journeys, He spoke to him and others through the local church.

In addition to God speaking through the church in Antioch, it was the church in Antioch who sent Saul and Barnabas. The Holy Spirit called them, but the local church sent them. The example we see throughout the New Testament is that God's people, in the power of the Holy Spirit, join in the work of the Holy Spirit. In Acts 13 we see the local church sending those whom the Holy Spirit has called. Today, though we have mission organizations that can be incredibly helpful, we must remember that they can never and should never replace the centrality of God's design for the local church in mission.

OUR CHURCH CAN HELP ASSESS OUR QUALIFICATIONS, CIRCUMSTANCES, GIFTINGS, AND DESIRES

Our local church should help assess whether we are biblically qualified for ministry. Some churches wisely require that all missionaries meet at least the biblical qualifications for deacons as set forth in 1 Timothy 3. A person sent out by the local church needs to be a maturing disciple who is ready to serve in and through the local church in the new context. Experience shows that the ranks of good church planters are going to be filled from the ranks of good church members. The Bible lays out a pattern of activity that shows how the disciples responded to the Great Commission. The missionary activity of the first disciples always included evangelism (sharing the gospel with nonbelievers), discipleship (teaching new disciples how to follow Jesus), and starting or strengthening churches. Their work centered around the church from start to finish. Therefore, if we are to follow their example, we must be biblically qualified to serve in the church.

Our church family can also help us assess our life circumstances and whether these circumstances should influence where, how, and even when we can serve. If you are married, you need to consider the needs and desires of your spouse. If you are a parent, you need to consider your responsibility to your children. If you have aging parents, you need to consider how you can honor your parents during this season of life. If you have financial debt, you need to consider how to manage that wisely. There is a possibility that due to previous choices and decisions, you may not be able to serve in certain roles quite yet or without careful consideration of your circumstances. For example, your preparation for missionary service may need to include considering education options for your children. Whatever your circumstance may be, the church can help you prayerfully consider how to steward the different aspects of your life well.

The local church also affirms the way God has uniquely equipped us to serve and strengthen the body of Christ. Each one of us has received a spiritual gift (or gifts) that we should use to serve one another (1 Pet. 4:10). We have been equipped to serve and should seek to use our spiritual gifts for the glory of God and for the equipping of His church. Our local church can observe our lives and help us discern how we are individually gifted. Some Christians take online spiritual gifts assessments as they seek to learn how God has gifted them. In my experience, the most effective assessments are often the observations and affirmations of those in our local church who see us using our gifts. If multiple people around us affirm a specific area of gifting, we should probably take note. Instead of determining your calling on your own, the first questions to ask are: "Does my church—the leadership and membership—see the same marks of the Lord's calling on my life? Does the church know me and affirm my qualification and giftedness enough to send me to proclaim the gospel and make disciples in places lacking access?"

Our church can help us consider our desires and affections. Paul tells us that it is not just permissible to aspire to minister to God's people, it's noble (1 Tim. 3:1). We are also encouraged to desire spiritual gifts that are given to equip and build up the body (1 Cor. 14:1–4). Yet not all of our desires are noble, and our deceitful hearts need the church to help us discern our motives and hearts. The church can help us train our hearts to delight in Jesus so that we desire what He does. The world tells us to "follow our hearts," but Scripture tells us that we can "lead our hearts" by prayerfully asking God to help us delight in Him and desire good things (Ps. 37:4). When we do this, we are transformed by the renewing of our minds, and we will be able to discern God's will (Rom. 12:2).

CONCLUSION

Remember the husband and wife who wanted to rejoin our work in Central Asia? They believed they were called to return to our team. Yet, after careful prayer, meditation on God's Word, and seeking counsel, the team on the ground decided they could not affirm the couple's decision to return. The local church that the couple would have joined on the field also did not affirm their decision to return. Therefore, we agreed that it would not be wise for them to rejoin that particular local ministry at that time. Since their external circumstances (you might say their external "call") didn't match their internal desires and sense of calling, we recommended they wait.

As for our family, we didn't find things lining up when we learned more about that work in Africa. If I'm being honest, we didn't desire to serve in Africa and the work didn't seem to fit with our training or our giftings. For that matter, we didn't end up in Europe or the Middle East either. God guided us through His Word and drew our hearts to a small city tucked away in a remote part of Central Asia. Our local church affirmed and confirmed this direction as well. After praying and fasting, we found a location and ministry that aligned with our circumstances and gifts where we knew we'd be able to proclaim the gospel and join in Christ's work of building His church where His name was not known.

The Holy Spirit does not speak audibly to most people. Yet God is still speaking and calling people to take the gospel to the nations. When the Bible, our internal desires, our external circumstances, and the church's affirmation all align, then it's a great indication to take the next step of faith and obedience. We prepare, we make ourselves ready, and we trust our great God to do the work. And we can trust Him completely because, as the apostle Paul told the church in Thessalonica, we know that "he who calls you is faithful; he will do it" (1 Thess. 5:24).

DISCUSS AND REFLECT

1. As you consider your role in missions, where do the Bible, your internal desires, your external circumstances, and the church's affirmation all align? Where might they not align?

2. What counsel does your local church give you as you prayerfully consider where and how to serve?

3. What character traits should you seek to develop as you prepare to serve as a missionary?

CHAPTER 2

Leaving What You Love

Hilary Alan

From the General Editor

I SAT ON THE balcony of my teammate's house with Hilary staring out at the Mediterranean one spring in North Africa. Hilary's husband, Curt, was serving as our sending church's missions pastor, and both he and Hilary had come to visit us. I don't remember much of the visit; however, we had one unique moment out on that balcony that has been seared into my mind.

The area in which we were living at the time had just been through the Arab Spring, and to say our city was "unstable" would have been an understatement. At that point in our journey, it was getting difficult for me to see beyond the tanks and the trash in the street, the gunshots and the stares of people I would pass by, and the long days of endless heat and tension.

There I was, though, sitting on a balcony with a person I did not know well, but whose story and life had garnered my respect and admiration. I was tired, trying to put on a strong face, but slightly envious of the fact that this lady in front of me got to get on a plane in a few days and go home. We made small talk for a bit, and then Hilary said something that hit me hard: "Emily, you have no idea how fortunate you are. This life you are living, you are so blessed."

What in the world? I thought. *Do you see my life? Do you see what we are dealing with every day? Nothing about this life could bear the hashtag "blessed."* It was hard for me to even take in the words she said. They were not said in reprimand or judgment, however. What Hilary saw around me was blessing even when I could not. We had followed God where He led. We said goodbye to what we loved and were straight in the middle of where God called us; therefore, we were blessed.

Hilary speaks volumes of wisdom as she shares the advice she has lived. I pray that God will use this to open your hands, which may be clutching hard to a few last things—and that you will be overwhelmed with a greater appreciation for all you are gaining as you follow Christ where He leads.

LEAVING WHAT YOU LOVE

> Then Jesus said to the Jews who had believed him, "If you continue in my word, you really are my disciples." (John 8:31)

"I love my life."

It has been eighteen years, and yet I remember exactly where I was and what I was doing when I had that thought just a few months before God would unexpectedly change my life and call my family to serve Him in Southeast Asia. At the time, going overseas to me meant taking a European vacation. Back then, I had every reason to love my life according to the world's standards. I had two thriving kids, a beautiful home, comfortable vacations, good friends, a solid church community, and my husband had a high-level position at "the best company to work for in America." What was there not to love? Though I called Elisabeth Elliot my spiritual mother at the time (and still do!), I thought being a missionary was a job for someone else. *Other* people were called to take the gospel to unreached areas, and my part was to enjoy reading about it.

And yet, in the midst of having achieved the American dream, my family and I found ourselves in the undeniable position of hearing the call of God to go to the other side of the world and facing the surrender of the life we had worked hard to build. If we were to obey that call, we would have to walk away from everything, just as you are now planning to do as well. And now as I write this, all these years later, I shudder to think what my life would be like had we not obeyed. It's funny to look back and think about what you thought you loved and what you thought was important when you discover something far better and far greater than you ever could have imagined.

Leaving what you love is a process. It is a profound exercise in learning to let go of many of the things in which we have been trained all our lives to look to provide comfort, peace, identity, and security. We are called to let go of our jobs, family, friends, routines, and all that is familiar and comfortable in response to the undeniable call of the One who is the source of true comfort, peace, identity, and security. Walking away from those things is not always easy. It is a transition that comes with moments of fear, anxiety, and doubt as we leave the familiar for so much that is unknown (see Nina's chapter for advice on that), but Scripture is very clear: leaving is part of the Christian life.

LET SCRIPTURE BE THE LOUDEST VOICE

I found that as I was preparing to leave, there were many voices stating their opinions about the road we were walking. Some of those voices were supportive, and some were not. Opinions came from family, friends, colleagues, and church members, but at times the loudest voice was the one inside my own head. *What if . . . Are we crazy? . . . I'm afraid to . . .* are thoughts that can wield a lot of power if you let them. Let me encourage you, though, as you prepare to leave what you love, let Scripture be the loudest voice. It is the only one that really matters because it is the only one that can be trusted. The Word is eternal, and thus its truth applies to—and extends even beyond—the circumstances in front of you. It is the only voice that will always tell you the truth. It is the only voice that will never lead you astray. It is also the one that will give you strength and confidence to keep walking, no matter what side of the world you find yourself on. If you are not abiding in God's Word, start doing it now. God says in John 8:31 that abiding in Jesus is the mark of a disciple. At times the Word of God will be the only thing that will sustain you. It will always be enough. It will never fail you. Abide in His Word.

The LORD said to Abram:

Go from your land,
your relatives,

and your father's house
to the land that I will show you.
I will make you into a great nation,
I will bless you,
I will make your name great,
and you will be a blessing. . . .

So Abram went, as the LORD had told him.
(Gen. 12:1–2, 4a)

It is in the Holy Scriptures that God calls His people to leave
over and over again throughout the Bible. Leaving is not just following the Good Shepherd in obedience, but also is an exercise
in following in the footsteps of our biblical ancestors. When I
wondered whether what we were doing was reckless because we
were in our forties and supposed to be "stable," it gave me incredible confidence to know that God was simply calling us to do just
what He had called Abram to do more than two thousand years
ago, and what He calls each one of His disciples to do ever since:
trust, obey, and follow.

Though it can be very appealing to think we are doing something very special when we go, we are not. There can be great
temptation as we leave to start to believe some of the kind words
that are spoken over us: *"What you are doing is amazing." "You are
giving up so much."* We and those around us may be tempted to
believe that we are doing something profoundly important, but as
Christians, according to what Scripture tells us, what we are doing
is actually profoundly normal.

Abraham, Joseph, Moses, Esther, Shadrach, Meshach,
Abednego, Daniel, every one of the disciples, and Jesus Himself

left their homes—some did so voluntarily, others due to circumstances beyond their control. And all over the world, believers are still doing that today. But as modern people who build their lives on earthly foundations that we convince ourselves represent security, we can succumb to the temptation to focus too much on "all that we are giving up," rather than the incredibly high and holy calling of being invited to follow in the steps of those who have gone before us.

Think of that for a moment: of all the work in the world that God could have chosen for us to participate in, He invited us into the work that *He* is doing. What an incredible privilege that is! Of course, as Christians, the ultimate "leaving what we love" happens at our conversion when we die to ourselves, take up our cross, and follow Him in faith and newness of life.

LISTEN TO THE WISDOM OF OTHERS WHO HAVE GONE BEFORE YOU

> Then Jesus said to his disciples, "If anyone wants
> to follow after me, let him deny himself, take up
> his cross, and follow me. For whoever wants to
> save his life will lose it, but whoever loses his life
> because of me will find it. For what will it benefit
> someone if he gains the whole world yet loses his
> life?" (Matt. 16:24–26a)

In following Christ, we often find it so difficult to leave what we love because when we dig down deep, we find we love our own will, our own desires, our own plans, and our own life more than we care to admit.

As I was preparing to leave, meditating on these verses in Genesis 12 and Matthew 16, to the point of memorizing them, helped me to focus my gaze upwards. They reminded me that in God's economy, what we were doing was normal, not extraordinary. They reminded me that if God had been calling His people to leave from the very beginning, then He must really know what He is doing in calling us now. Scripture teaches us that, for the disciple, there is only one response when Jesus says, "Follow Me," and that is the immediate dropping of your own plans. Otherwise, He isn't your Lord.

But I also found encouragement in focusing my gaze horizontally. Reading biographies of other sent ones made me feel less alone and gave me a sense of fellowship and community with others who had gone before me, even decades earlier. I can't wait to meet Ann Judson and Betty Scott Stam in heaven. It was humbling to read about others who admittedly went under much more challenging circumstances than we were facing. It made me appreciate the privilege of traveling by airplane rather than ship, having access to technology to stay in close touch with loved ones rather than the occasional letter, and other comforts that come with being sent during modern times. I read their stories over and over. I thought, *If God was faithful to them, then I can trust that He will be faithful to me.* When I struggled to press on, their stories made me feel like I could keep taking the next step of obedience.

But despite all of the encouragement that comes from those who have gone before me, the flesh is strong. It's not just lifestyle and modern comforts that we find ourselves surrendering; our relationships, our "what ifs," our plans are just as powerful.

Once again, by abiding in His Word, we can find precedent and comfort.

TRUST GOD WITH THE ONES YOU LOVE THE MOST

> "And everyone who has left houses or brothers or sisters or father or mother or children or fields because of my name will receive a hundred times more and will inherit eternal life." (Matt. 19:29)

Jesus is well aware of everything He is asking you to leave. He knew this was going to happen because He is the one who called you and the one directing your steps. How do we know? He told us in His Word, before we were ever born.

The first time we served overseas, I thought I surrendered everything. Surrendering everything was hard. After all, we'd sold our home and belongings, quit our jobs, and left our supportive community—what else was there to let go of? And then after a season back in the U.S. on staff at our church, God called us to go again—but this time without our beloved kids to whom we are very close and who were by then both adults. To be honest, responding in obedience to that call was so much harder and took me a little longer to surrender because the cost seemed higher. My confidence in leaving the second time is the confidence I share with you for the loved ones you may have to leave behind: God sees them all the time, He is with them, and He loves them far better than you ever could because He loved them first. Yes, you can trust Him even with them. That absolute assurance that the Father sees was my confidence to get on the plane the second time.

I hope it will be yours as well. Our part is to trust, obey, and go where He sends us.

It can be hard to be the sent one and to leave family members behind, whether because you love them and will miss them, or because sometimes parents or family members are not supportive. I speak with experience from both perspectives. When I was sent, I did not have supportive parents, but when my son was sent, I was a supportive parent. Both positions can be hard. But I exhort you with this wisdom that my pastor spoke over me years ago, which I have never forgotten: *You honor your mother and father when you become the man or woman that God created you to be.* Whether your parents are supportive or not, you can go in obedience to your Father, and as a parent we can send our children in that same obedience.

To honor your parents from afar, I suggest that you invite them into the entire process of leaving what you love right at the start. Ask them to pray with and for you as you prepare to leave. Share with them what you are learning in the process of God preparing and equipping you to go. If you are invited to speak to groups before you leave, invite your parents to attend the meetings. Watching and listening to you tell others where you are going and why can be a powerful experience for your family members.

Once you are in your assigned location, make time for regular communication and share with them what you are experiencing. Ask them to pray for you and with you for the people you are trying to reach. Invite them to visit you on the field if they are able and "come and see" the work that you are engaged in. In doing so, you make your parents supporting members of your team on the ground. This is not just an opportunity for you and your team to receive support, but a discipleship opportunity for your parents as they engage in new work, pray for a people they previously may have never considered, and maybe most important of all, have a front-row seat to watch God work in and through their child in new ways. Walking alongside someone who is trusting, obeying, and following helps us to have the courage to do likewise. And remember that leaving what you love is a process that your parents may very well be going through as well as they prepare to send someone they love into something very unknown.

This is not always an easy process for you as the sent one, nor is it easy for your family. You can expect to encounter at least some discouragement or distraction as you prepare to leave what you love. Then you can expect it to happen again and again when you get to where you are going. Now is the time to prepare for those unwelcome occurrences. I encourage you, as you abide in His Word, to decide now on some "anchor verses" for yourself—Scriptures that, every time you read them, pull you up out of your own circumstances and point you right back to Jesus. They will be a lifeline for you. We each have personal, intimate relationships with Jesus, so your anchor verses will be different ones than mine. Find the ones that slay or encourage your heart every time. You're going to need them. There will be days when Scripture will be all you have to feel encouraged. But rest assured it is more than sufficient to remind you who you are, why you are there, and Who is helping you, every single day.

BEFORE YOU LEAVE, THANK THE FATHER FOR HIS FAITHFULNESS

Before you leave, no matter what side of the world you are on, whether you are coming or going, I encourage you to practice something I taught my own children to do. Having moved multiple times, they have lived their entire lives leaving behind places, people, and things that they love as God continues to call us all to different places of service. Before you go, and yes, this applies to before you leave America, find a place that is meaningful to you, and spend some time there giving thanks to God for His faithfulness to you in that place. No matter what has happened in that place, God has been faithful to you. That's His character. Regardless of the circumstances, He has been with you, and He has provided for you, and He is always at work in and through you. He sees you. He knows you. He loves you. Turn your gaze toward Him and take the time to give thanks before you get on the plane. Before you leave, thank Him.

You might also make time to thank significant people in your life who have helped encourage you, mold you, and shape you. Thank them whether or not they are supportive of your decision to go. If they have played a part in your discipleship process, if they have fed you, housed you, prayed for you, or listened to you, make a point to thank them.

One thing that you can't see now and that may surprise you is this: by God's grace you may find that the place where you are going, whether you are going for the short term or the long, when and if it becomes time to return to America, you may find leaving *there* harder than it was to leave here. That was the case for me, and that was something I never expected, and that no one prepared me for. In leaving what I love to serve in new places, among new people, experiencing new cultures, my sense of "home" has expanded. It's amazing to look back and now have multiple places around the world that I can call one of my many homes and many new people to love and pray with and for. "I love my life" has become "I love the Lord who has my life. And I am grateful for the privilege of having a small part in the eternal work that God is doing."

That doesn't mean that hard things didn't happen. They did. And hard things will happen to you too. But remember that hard things also happen in America, and God promises to use them all. We are in the hands of a faithful and trustworthy God. Leaving what you love well sets you up for arriving well, and arriving well sets you up for serving well.

Often missionaries, as they prepare to leave what they love, do their best to bring along a lot of what they love. Yes, it's important to bring a few things from home. But avoid the temptation to take up precious room in your suitcase with things like packets of ranch dressing mix. You are going to a place where you are going to learn to love new things as God begins His work of changing you and yoking your heart to the place and the people He has called you to. By the time we were preparing to return to the States at the end of our first assignment, we were giving away the things from our home country that we had brought over or had sent over because, at the time, "we just had to have them." The longer we were there, the less important those things became. Now I'm very thankful for Asian markets in America, places I never shopped at before leaving.

SAY GOODBYE WELL

The last bit of wisdom I have to share with you was spoken over me during our weeks of formal preparation by our sending agency. They told us to take care of any unfinished business with anyone before we leave. I'm so grateful for wise people who can think for us and who have so much more experience than we do. If there is anything that needs to be said, make a point to say it before you go. If there is anyone you need to meet with or to reconcile with, make the time. You know what is unfinished. You will be so glad you took care of whatever it is before you leave.

Finally, here's a little secret that is very counterintuitive: letting go of what you love is a good thing. In releasing things that feel very important, you free up space in your heart for more of what truly matters: Jesus. Consider it a privilege, not a sacrifice, to let go. When you get on the plane, make sure all you have to do is go. Don't be like the rich young ruler who, when he learned the cost of following Jesus, is described as being "dismayed by this demand" (Mark 10:21–22). Remember that it is Jesus who asks for your life. The people you are going to live among did not ask you to come nor did they ask you to give up anything to live there, so do not bring a *"Do you know what I gave up for you?"* spirit to them. It is, however, okay to feel like you are stepping off a cliff when you get on the plane. Courageous steps of faith require just that: *courage.*

I'll end with these words from our sister and missionary forerunner, Amy Carmichael. She left what she loved in Ireland at the age of twenty-four and served in Japan and India for fifty-five years without ever returning "home." God grew her heart to love a new country, new people, and new work, and her legacy continues today, decades later. She could never have imagined what God would do in and through her life when she left her home, never to return, because she made a new home somewhere else. Her words are mine for you as you prepare to leave what you love:

> But this I know: you will regret nothing when you look back, except lack of faith or fortitude or love. You will never regret having thrown all to the winds in order to follow your Master and Lord. Nothing will seem too much to have done or suffered, when, in the end, we see Him and the marks of His wounds; nothing will ever seem enough. Even the weariness of deferred hope will be forgotten, in the joy that is not of earth.[6]

DISCUSS AND REFLECT

1. In the Gospels of Matthew and Mark, when Jesus calls His disciples to "follow," we are told that they dropped their nets *immediately* and *followed* in response. Why do you think we find this call so much more difficult to be immediately obedient to? What is hardest for you to be obedient to Jesus's call on your life?

2. The author describes how leaving home to follow God is something not radical but normal. What are some practical steps you can take to "normalize" leaving? How does this change our perspectives as we prepare to leave?

3. The author lists several biblical figures who left their homes or possessions to follow God's call. Is there one that stands out to you? Why?

4. What are some of your "anchor verses?" How did the Lord first impress them upon your heart?

CHAPTER 3

---- -- --- -- -- --- --- -- -- -- -- -- -- -- -- --- ---

SERVING WELL AS A TEAM

C. J. Olivia

From the General Editor

THE LORD GIFTED me with two precious years of getting to walk side by side with C. J. We did not know C. J. and her husband well before they joined our team. However, like most overseas relationships, we were deeply bonded within a handful of months. C. J and I shared a love for running and exploring culture. She is an incredibly curious and emotionally intelligent human. She constantly pushed me both to think well and to love others well.

The two years I had with her were not easy years for me personally. I was spiritually, emotionally, and physically exhausted by many life circumstances during that season. In His kind providence, God provided for so many of my needs by placing C. J. on my team during those two years. She showed up as a listening ear when God prompted. She gave me new eyes to see the culture when it felt like the eyes I had were failing me. She loved my kids unconditionally, no matter what side of themselves they showed her. It was truly a joy to be on a team with C. J. and her husband.

37

Since our paths parted, she and her family have also stepped into leadership of a team in Europe serving Middle Eastern people. She has wisdom to share as one who has served under the leadership of another and also as one who has been asked to lead others. For these reasons and more, I am excited to have her contributing this chapter on teaming. I am praying that her words would encourage, convict, and spur you on to the sacrificial love it takes to team well.

BEING A STRONG TEAM

I'll never forget the day our plane landed in North Africa. At the time, the country was under a military-enforced curfew, and everyone had to be in their homes by 7:00 p.m. We landed in the middle of the night and in the middle of the imposed lockdown. My husband and I were twenty-two at the time. It was our first move overseas, and we didn't know one word of the local language. We were exhausted from travel and from tearful goodbyes with our family at the airport. Yet here we were in the dead of night in a van headed to our new home. In our state of delirium, I remember being pulled over, doors flung open, and looking up to rifles in our faces by the police officers looking for our documentation. We had been in the country for thirty minutes, and we were already eager to turn back around and fly home. The details of that night are unforgettably etched in our memories, but what sticks out to me the most is surprisingly not the guns pointed in our faces or the fires of protest blazing along the roads. The most profound memory of that experience was the two peanut butter and jelly sandwiches clutched in our hands.

We definitely did not have an appetite after thirty-six hours of airplane food, but our new team leader met us at the airport with sandwiches in hand. His wife had made peanut butter and jelly sandwiches and stocked our kitchen with things that would be "familiar" to us when we arrived. She had scrubbed our floors to get one layer of African dust off. She had washed a set of sheets and had freshly made our bed so we could easily collapse into bed after two days of travel.

Our life in North Africa didn't necessarily get easier from there. But when the people around you are anticipating needs you didn't know you had, you grow in your sustainability and resilience to walk through those hard situations.

This is the gift of being on a team in cross-cultural work.

Team relationships in an overseas context are unlike any other I have experienced. It is impossible to truly define them. You take on the roles of friends, coworkers, church members, and family members. You fill multiple roles in one another's lives. In a Stateside context, these roles are typically spread across hundreds of people. On an overseas team, three or four people play all of these necessary roles. This dynamic creates a great deal of pressure on a small group of people. But it also presents a tremendous opportunity to live in deep community when we approach it the way God intends.

THE SUPPLIER OF YOUR SOUL

Therefore, since we have a great high priest who has passed through the heavens—Jesus the Son of God—let us hold fast to our confession. For we do not have a high priest who is unable to sympathize with our weaknesses, but one who has been tempted in every way as we are, yet without sin. Therefore, let us approach the throne of grace with boldness, so that we may receive mercy and find grace to help us in time of need. (Heb. 4:14–16)

When we think about teamwork from the perspective of Scripture, many passages may come to mind. The above passage in Hebrews stands out as particularly appropriate in regard to teaming according to biblical design. These verses have been foundational as I have navigated team relationships, whether in conflict or in harmony, whether as a team member or a team leader.

It's easy to feel isolated while living overseas, even on a team. You are living thousands of miles away from home. You are on a different continent and living in an unfamiliar language. You become aware of needs and feelings that you have never had before. Overseas life has a way of leaving our hearts naked and exposed. Without even realizing it, we can begin to think our situation is unique and no one understands us. We can easily project these aches in our own hearts onto our team and think, "It must be their fault I feel this way."

Your team will fail you at some point. Your team will disappoint you. Your team will not meet certain expectations or needs that you have. But Christ—our Advocate, our High Priest— understands. He can sympathize *in every way*, and we can draw near to Him. We receive grace from Christ in our time of need. Even when our teams let us down, Christ is supplying our heart's deepest needs. I have seen this truth become foundational for healthy relationships on our teams. And I have found it to be true whether one is leading or following.

Healthy team relationships always stem from individuals abiding in and drawing on their relationship with the Lord. When we daily (and some days, hourly) approach the throne of grace, we find Jesus ready to sympathize with all of our weaknesses and shortcomings. This then frees us not to look to what our teams are or are not providing us, but to the only One who can truly supply the needs of our soul. When we believe that Christ can sympathize *in every way*, we begin to experience a hope and security in our hearts. When we experience Jesus's grace and mercy for ourselves, we can then extend it to our team.

Because Christ deals gently with us, we can deal gently with our teammates. This is essential for our ministry overseas and for healthy team dynamics. We can't offer others what we don't first possess in our hearts. If we are insecure, we will look to our teammates for security. If we are discontent in our hearts, we will begin, sometimes unknowingly, to project that onto our team. We will never be perfect or have perfect teammates. It's imperative that we do the heart work before the Lord, daily reminding our hearts that He understands and He sympathizes with us. He asks us to draw near, and He alone brings rest to our souls. He pours grace over us, so that we can pour grace into our teams. He extends mercy to our wayward hearts, so we can turn our eyes away from ourselves and fix our eyes on Him.

Only when we are looking to the Lord alone to meet our deepest needs will we be able to remove that expectation from the shoulders of those around us. Only when we are looking to the Lord alone to meet our deepest needs will we be able to serve, love, and enjoy our teammates. Only then can we serve and love the people we are ministering to. Jesus is our Advocate. He understands fully. He sympathizes in every way with us. Let us draw these gifts from Christ and let us be these to one another on our teams. As Christ has been to us, may we be to one another—both for the longevity of the work we want to see God accomplish and for the glory of God. May God look at our team relationships and receive glory. May our local friends look at our team relationships and see the steadfast love of the Lord.

THE GREATEST GIFT YOU COULD BRING YOUR TEAM IS YOUR RELATIONSHIP WITH CHRIST

Healthy team relationships always stem from individuals abiding in and drawing on their relationship with the Lord. When Christ supplies our every need (Phil. 4:19), we can then enjoy our team relationships and not look to them to provide things that only God was meant to supply. Hopefully, your team will also meet the needs you have. As brothers and sisters in Christ, we find joy in serving and loving one another sacrificially.

It can be easy in an overseas context to become spiritually depleted. You are more fatigued than you have ever been. You don't have the same church service that has fed you for so many years. You don't have the weekly Bible study or small group or church event. Because our teammates are sometimes the only people in the entire city that even speak the same language, it can be easy to look to them for our spiritual growth. God willing, they will be a piece of your spiritual growth, but they cannot be primary. You have to learn how to feed your soul. It is paramount to our team relationships that we each, team members and team leaders, draw our hope and joy and purpose from the finished work of Jesus.

The deeper you abide in Christ, the more you will enjoy your team, extend grace when there is error, and feel connected in your team's community. The greatest way to serve your team and team leaders is to bring and cultivate a deep, abiding relationship with the Lord.

THERE IS NO PERFECT TEAM

No two teams look the same. Some teams spend all their free time together. Other teams approach ministry more individually. Some teams may find and join an existing local church. Other teams opt to form their own house church. Some teams vacation together. Others might travel individually.

We were once married with no kids serving on a team. We are now team leaders with three young kids. Chances are your team members will represent a diversity of seasons of life. Singles and married with no kids will have a vastly different pace of life and schedule than families with kids. Families with older kids will have different needs than families with young kids. When we are spiritually healthy, we can look at that diversity and praise God for how it represents the church. When we are unhealthy, we start to believe the grass is greener somewhere else. We start to believe the location or the team (or the weather or the language or the culture . . .) is the problem and not the discontentment in our hearts. This is one of the greatest challenges I fight in my own heart while living overseas. When I begin to project my discontentment to the things around me, I know it's a good indicator to look inward and ask the Lord to reveal things that I am allowing to supply my soul's needs outside of Himself.

When we were living in North Africa, the heat was a stressor for me. There is something profoundly sanctifying about sweating while you sleep. Now that we are living in Europe, the winter is a stressor for me. It is cold and dark for a very long time. On my good days, I can look at this objectively and see that no matter the climate, my heart is prone to compare and complain. In spite of what I now have, I long for something more or different. It isn't my context that is the problem; it is my heart.

When we were living in North Africa with no kids, it was easy to think, *If I just had kids, ministry would be easier or team relationships would become more similar.* In our current location with three young kids, it is easy to think, *If we had fewer kid responsibilities, we would be better team leaders and have more time for ministry.*

This deceptive trap of comparison can easily steal joy from your team. There is no perfect team. There will always be a "better" context or a "better" team. Each person on your team is in a God-given season. There will always be the lure of the "ideal." But when we approach team as a gift to enjoy, not a perfect savior to all our problems, we will start to love and appreciate our teams.

DON'T EXPECT YOUR GIFTINGS TO BE YOUR TEAM LEADERS' GIFTINGS

The body of Christ is beautiful when each member is using the gifts the Holy Spirit brought together on your particular team. We all bring unique strengths. We also bring unique weaknesses. It is easy to notice the things we do well but focus our attention on what other people don't do well. We often expect our team or team leaders to serve us in the way we want to be served. But just like any relationship, those dynamics take time and often conflict to grow and develop.

You might be a natural includer—someone who is always inviting more people to the party. Your teammate or team leader might not have that gifting. This may leave you thinking your team leader doesn't want community. In reality, your leader's approach to community is just really different than yours. Their gifting may be better demonstrated in smaller groups, going deeper in relationships rather than wider.

We've also seen how living in a cross-cultural context changes your personality in a lot of ways. Living in a foreign language and culture takes a significant amount of energy. I have seen myself become much more introverted the longer I have lived overseas. Stepping into foreign cultures and languages is exhausting. Everything feels harder than it was before. It's important to remember this in our team relationships and further highlights the need to extend grace to our teams as we are all navigating new things both in ourselves and in the surroundings around us. The first few years overseas you are relearning who you are, and that has a profound impact on your team relationships.

Learning and growing together in the ways God has gifted us starts with our relationship with the Lord. We can have conflict and extend grace to one another. We can learn from our experiences and our mistakes. We can learn patience as we ask the Lord to grow our hearts together. It's impossible not to bring expectations to your team. Expectations can be really good and God-given, but if we can't open our hands and let go of unmet expectations, we will kill the community of our teams. We will continue to feel disappointed with the people God put on our team when they don't measure up to the ideals in our heads. When you can open your hands with your own giftings, you will then be able to enjoy the diversity of gifts on your team. Only then will you enjoy the fullness of what team relationships can be.

FILL GAPS WITH TRUST

When we are tired and depleted, small things have a way of seeming much bigger. Team relationships provide plenty of opportunities to assume the worst of your teammate.

I remember when we were brand-new team leaders, we had just moved back overseas with our eighteen-month-old and I was twenty-weeks pregnant with our second baby. We had zero language and no knowledge of our new city. We honestly felt like we were drowning for the first three years in this city. We stumbled through team leadership. Right when we got our feet under us, we had our third baby. We didn't communicate well with our new teammates that we were overwhelmed in these seasons, and this left them feeling isolated, thinking we didn't want to spend time with them.

This was a major growing opportunity for our team. We had to extend grace to one another and believe that we all were for one another, even when it didn't feel that way. If I had to cancel plans, I had the confidence to believe they understood my season of life and it wasn't because I didn't enjoy time with them. When other teammates planned trips together and we didn't go, we knew it wasn't because they didn't want us to join, but because travel at our kids' ages isn't actually a vacation.

Work hard to assume the best of your teammates and team leaders instead of letting it feed negativity in your heart.

Your leader or your teammate will inevitably fail and disappoint you at some point. They will forget to communicate something or not invite you to something you wanted to be a part of. There will be a time when you will feel overlooked, unappreciated, disrespected, or left out. Additionally, an overseas context brings new stressors and unexpected tensions into our day-to-day lives. Things that were once simple, like buying groceries or walking down the street, may now take a full day's effort. Our baseline of stress is higher than it used to be. As you can imagine, this can lead to living in a state of frustration.

Cross-cultural living is hard. It's so easy to project these frustrations toward the people closest to you—your team. Insignificant things that didn't irritate you in your home country will irritate you overseas. Instead of letting these things push you further from one another, let them deepen your team relationships by extending trust and grace.

When there is a gap of understanding with a team member, it can either be an opportunity to extend grace or to fuel suspicion. Work hard to fill the gaps of understanding with patience and grace. Only the Holy Spirit can do that in you, but that is why your effort to draw from the mercy and grace of Jesus will free you to enjoy and love your team well. Team dynamics are unlike any other relationship in the world. What an opportunity to put the glory of God on display!

THE GIFT OF TEAM

There is nothing special about peanut butter and jelly sandwiches, but for me they will always remind me of the gift of being on a team. Healthy teams are made up of sinful brothers and sisters in Christ who are committed to loving the Lord with all their heart, soul, mind, and strength. From that foundation, teams can love and serve one another.

It might be dropping off a meal during a hard week for a teammate. It might be offering a ride to alleviate a stressful commute. It might be watching a kid for an afternoon to give a parent a break. It might be sitting on the floor of a living room to just be a listening ear.

My family has walked through a diversity of seasons overseas. We've birthed babies, had traumatic accidents with our kids, and endured many, many stomach bugs. We have braved new foods and fumbled through so many language barriers. We've made our fair share of cultural mistakes, and we've had too many awkward conversations to count.

Do you know who have fielded those good, hard, scary, tearful, and hilarious moments in our life? The small group of people God has gifted us in each season. Our team has changed from year to year and the faces are not always the same, but God has been faithful to provide community around us to navigate the life He has called us to—through a team.

Following and leading on a team can look so many different ways. In various seasons, serving your team well will look differently. There will be seasons when you will feel poured into and there will be seasons when you don't. When you are committed to abiding deeply in the presence of Christ, you will be able to navigate those changes alongside a team that is invested in one another as God knits your hearts together in Him. You will be a joy to your teammates and to your team leaders.

Do the work to take care of your soul. That is the greatest gift you could bring to your team. Whether leading or being led, seek the Lord and serve one another.

DISCUSS AND REFLECT

1. What are some expectations you have for your team and your team leaders? How much time do you expect to spend together?

2. What giftings do you think God has given you to serve your team? How might those giftings look different in an overseas context?

3. What does a typical week look like for your team? What do holidays look like for your team? What does church look like?

CHAPTER 4

Prayer and Evangelism

Lydia Pettus

From the General Editor

THE MISSIONARY WORLD extends around the entire globe, yet it often feels surprisingly small. It is not at all uncommon to hear names and stories of other missionaries working in other fields whom you have not met. And often, if you wait long enough, you will have opportunity to cross paths with each other.

This is what happened with the author of this chapter and me. From time to time, I had heard amazing things about the ministry of a woman named Lydia. As I was preparing a list of contributors for this book, I had the honor of meeting her virtually to discuss this project. Even though we had never met in person, I immediately felt like I knew her due to the fact that I had heard stories about her for years. She also has a way of making strangers feel like old friends due to her warmth, her genuine love for the Lord, and her welcoming smile. It also helped that we share many common connections and both knew stories about each other before getting to meet. Geography has separated us until now, but by God's grace, our worlds have overlapped for a time.

Outside of her friendly and outgoing disposition, two things immediately stood out to me about Lydia. The first thing is that Lydia has given a clear priority to spending time with the Lord in prayer. In our first conversation together, she shared much about her ministry of prayer for the nations, and it was clear that she believes that God hears and answers.

The second thing that I couldn't help but notice is that she has a heart and a passion to share the gospel with whomever God puts in her life. After becoming a believer and working in the U.S. for a season, God led her to Southeast Asia, Central Asia, and now back to the States. In each of these very different settings, Lydia has dedicated herself to evangelism and to training evangelists. Lydia loves the Lord, loves the gospel, and longs to see believers equipped to proclaim the gospel in order that the nations would be glad. I am so excited for you to glean from her wisdom, commitment, and encouragement to us as we consider the task of evangelism among the nations.

PRAYER AND EVANGELISM

I sat on the edge of a stunningly beautiful island. The island was lush with palm trees, and it was surrounded by crystal-blue water that was clear enough to see the colorful fish swimming all around from my shaded spot on the beach. Surrounding me on every side were the sun-soaked faces of people I would soon come to love. What a gift I had been given to live with and among these people in this place.

With the gift, though, came a certain heaviness. Most of these beautiful people, though created in the image of God, were people who had never heard of God's beautiful plan of salvation. Jesus Christ had come in the form of a man, fully human and fully divine, to cleanse them of their sins and give them new life. God loved them so much, but they had no idea.

In the meticulous sovereignty of God's plan, He had allowed me to be a bearer of that message in that place. What a grave privilege it was.

As I sat in front of an oscillating fan, drying off the beads of sweat with every rotation, not knowing my surroundings or even how to speak the language, I thought, *Lord, is this really what You want me to do?* Though my questions were marked by timidity and contained a twinge of fear, I really was excited and ready. I was in the middle of God's command to "go." I had left behind the familiar and was exactly where He wanted me. I could not have asked for more.

Looking back, I can see that for years God had been preparing me to "go." I can hear the tune of the hymn "Grace, Grace, God's Grace" as I think back to the faithful people with whom He had surrounded me as I developed in my walk with Christ. The Lord had placed me in the midst of men and women who demonstrated for me what it looked like to proclaim God's message of good news to those who needed to hear it. These were people who had the gospel constantly and joyfully on their lips, ready to share at all times. Observing their surrender to God's will pushed me to commit to follow Jesus and "do likewise" (Luke 10:37b ESV) in whatever situations He called me to.

In His goodness and sovereignty, God wasted nothing in my life. Early on in my walk with Him, my desire to follow His commands led me to help start a church in Virginia alongside other committed believers. These people discipled me in the rhythms of a deep and growing relationship with God that was evidenced by both personal holiness and gospel proclamation. While our community surely had plenty of its own lostness that we hoped to impact with our church plant, it was my fellow church planters who also introduced me to the reality that there were people in other countries who did not have access to the Scriptures. While reaching out to our local community, they did not fail to remember the many around the world who have never heard the name of Jesus.

The reality of what that meant stung my heart. Millions and millions of people would live the entirety of their lives without access to the knowledge of the God who had created them. They did not know that God loves them, and they did not see His love on display as He sent His Son to save them. They lived in His world and they bore His image, yet they did not know. And unless someone went to tell them, they would remain separated from Him for all of eternity. Gut-wrenching.

After having my eyes opened to the fact that there were millions of unreached and unengaged people around the world, I found it difficult to go about my life in the usual casual matter. I knew God was calling me to go.

So, I went. God led me to Southeast Asia, and I went with the commands of Matthew 28 in my heart and as my badge. I was going to go to make disciples of all nations by baptizing them in the triune name of our God and by teaching them to obey all that

Jesus taught His disciples (vv. 19–20). Truthfully, I probably was overconfident regarding my ability to tell people this good news. I knew it was necessary and that God commanded me to do it. How hard could it be? I just need to tell them, right?

As I arrived, I was immediately put in my place by the mere fact that everything around me was unfamiliar. The heat was suffocating. The people were as unsure of what to do with me as I was of them. I had absolutely no idea how to speak, listen, read, or write. I walked differently, looked differently, ate differently. I was a scene. How was I supposed to do the task I had been commissioned to do? I had naively expected to get off the plane, share the good news, and watch people turn and repent in joy. Instead, what I found was heat, sweat, funny stares, and a realization that I had no ability on my own power to carry out the Great Commission.

Thankfully, the promise that Jesus gave in Matthew 28:20 held true. He was with me. He had not left me to myself to carry out His work. Despite my newfound and ever-growing awareness of my inabilities to do what I had come to do, the Holy Spirit's presence comforted me and reminded me of Jesus's authoritative encouragement "to walk and pray and tell" as a means of making disciples among these people.

BY MYSELF AND YET NOT ALONE

The team I came to join was small. When I say "small," I mean that it consisted of me and my team leaders. They lived in the capital city, and not long after I arrived, we discerned that the Lord was leading me to move to a town six hours away. We made this decision because we knew of a need for an English teacher there. So, I went. I got settled and after two days in the new town, new house, and new neighborhood, my team leaders said their goodbyes and returned to their city.

I was a twenty-eight-year-old woman living completely alone, with my closest known contacts now six hours away and a phone number of a man who could answer questions should the need arise. Unfortunately, I was also keenly aware that the conservative Muslim environment around me made it very inappropriate for me—a single, foreign woman—to actually call this man unless it was an absolute emergency.

I had felt plenty helpless in the capital city with my team leaders as my only friends. Now in this new city, I felt even more useless. I will admit to even being frustrated at times. I just wanted to share the gospel. That was why I had given up all I had back home to come. Yet, here I was, all alone in a place where my language was not even strong enough to go to the market to buy an egg or an apple. How was I to share the reality of the atoning sacrifice of Christ?

Out of desperation, I read the Word of God and prayed constantly. God used that time in His Word, in His presence, and in the struggle to teach me the power of simple, daily obedience. He changed my heart to realize that I was not supposed to take the Great Commission and wear it as a badge, fulfilling it out of my own strength and ability.

He had asked me to "go." But I was not to go on my own strength, but by the power of His Spirit working in me. I was to walk in obedience in proclamation while I rested in His power to change hearts. Though I had read 2 Corinthians 12:9 a thousand times before I left the U.S., it was here on the mission field that I learned and understood—quite possibly for the first time—how God chooses to use our frailties for His purposes.

He taught me that to proclaim His truth to the nations, it must flow from a heart that daily interacts with Him, strives to know His Word, and abides in prayer. The commands of Matthew 28 still gripped me, but as I walked through those early days on the field, leaning desperately on the Holy Spirit, I began to understand how dependent prayer must undergird evangelism.

These convictions about prayer and evangelism came to life through my experience of helpless dependence. But in my time in the Word during those early years, I began to see how these principles were present in the Bible long before they were discovered on the field. Let me share with you some of the encouragement that I found in the Word as I sought to pursue prayer-fueled evangelism.

PRAYERS AND PROCLAMATION

Books about missions cannot help but discuss Paul's life and ministry. He is seen as the prototype for contemporary missions by many. His desire to preach the gospel where Christ has not been named is the inherited heartbeat of many a modern missionary. His letters are chock-full of missionary wisdom. Naturally, then, I have spent a lot of time poring over Paul's words as he defends, describes, and urges others to follow him in his missionary efforts.

One place I have found encouragement is in Paul's letters to Timothy, his son in the faith, as he passes along instructions for life and ministry to his young disciple. For example, in 1 Timothy 2:1–4, Paul writes:

First of all, then, I urge that petitions, prayers, intercessions, and thanksgivings be made for everyone, for kings and all those who are in authority, so that we may lead a tranquil and quiet life in all godliness and dignity. This is good, and it pleases God our Savior, who wants everyone to be saved and to come to the knowledge of the truth.

In these verses Paul is continuing a line of thought he began in the first chapter regarding how we are to "fight the good fight, having faith and a good conscience" (1 Tim. 1:18–19). Here he explains the role of prayer in fighting the good fight. He beckons his readers to pray in many ways, for everyone, as we go about our daily lives, abiding in Christ; all of these prayers are part of how we are to "fight the good fight."

Why does Paul encourage this? He states that it is good and pleasing to God because He wants everyone to know the truth (1 Tim. 2:3–4). It would seem, then, that Paul expects our prayers to precede and pervade our work of proclamation. God desires all to grasp, believe, and cherish this gospel. Paul expects us to connect our prayer and our proclamation.

In addition to the efficacy of prayers for those with whom we will share the gospel, there are also practical benefits to intentional, evangelism-preparing prayers. By praying in these ways and for these people, we focus our mind on God and His desires. In so doing, we find ourselves less concerned to dwell on our surrounding circumstances. Praying for God's saving mercy to be poured out on those around us also naturally inclines us toward living tranquil and quiet lives with godliness and dignity.

Instead of focusing on the difficulties of cross-cultural relationship or second-language communication, these prayers refocus us on what God—by His sovereign power—longs to do in the lives of our neighbors. This reminds us that it is His will, His work, and His power that will work through us. Such prayers take the pressure of convincing someone to believe off of our language skills and reasoning ability and place them on God, who has already told us that He desires them to come to faith.

Prayer is essential to our task as missionaries. God hears and loves our big, seemingly impossible-to-answer prayers. He wants us to bring Him our specific prayers, those we whisper into the noisy crowds while prayer walking, and our Scripture-soaked prayers that will serve to remind us of His sovereign intentions to be known by the nations. All of these prayers are used by His mighty hand to open doors of opportunity. These opportunities may come through conversations with our backyard neighbors, or they may come through formal interactions with those in high levels of authority. Dependent prayer refocuses us and also prepares us to see where God is working around us so that we might be ready to do the work of proclamation even in unlikely circumstances—whether in the early stages of arriving and acclimating, or in the intimidating offices of magistrates and authority figures.

While prayer is necessary, we do need to note that praying for evangelistic opportunities is not yet evangelism itself. Evangelism is the proclamation of the gospel of Jesus Christ. When we engage in evangelism in a missionary context, we are almost always doing it in places where Christ is unknown or under-proclaimed. To evangelize, we must be able to explain and reason with people that Jesus Christ is the Son of God. We must be able to communicate that He was sent to earth to take on human flesh and to live a perfect life in obedience to the Father. We need to be able to show them in Scripture that He willingly sacrificed Himself to forgive and cleanse people of their sins. We must be able to articulate that He died but then was victoriously raised to life on the third day. And we must be clear to say that He is now seated at the right hand of God the Father, serving as our great High Priest.

This is our message. This is good news that we have to share. But in order for it to be good news, it must be proclaimed and explained. We need to be able to invite people to see it and read it for themselves in the pages of Scripture. True evangelism will require us to do the hard work of language learning, of gaining cultural understanding, and of relationship building. Evangelism is dependent upon the Holy Spirit and must be precipitated by prayer. But it is not complete until this message of what God has done in Christ is proclaimed and people are invited to repent and believe. I realized that for me to discharge my Matthew 28 calling, I needed to be a person of both prayer and proclamation.

Dear reader, I wish that I could sit down over coffee or tea with you and tell you all I wish I had known before I left for the field so many years ago. However, with this last section, let me just touch on a few practical things that I learned about prayer and evangelism while on the field. I hope that these will help you to see the natural wedding of prayer and proclamation as the rubber hits the road and you land wherever the Lord places you.

PRAY

Prayer is the foundation of proclamation. Proclamation done without the intercession of the Spirit is an exercise of relying on our own abilities. Apart from the Spirit's work, we cannot change hearts. This is a sobering reality that must drive us to prayer. On the field I prayed continually that God would give me eyes to see people He desired me to share with—a habit I have continued in my new neighborhood back home. When I was in Southeast Asia, it often involved praying while walking. When I was in an extremely closed country where I could not walk by myself, I prayed while driving and prayed while in the marketplace. All of this is based on the knowledge that God loves to answer our prayers expressed in faith according to His will. As you meet with women—and even as you prepare to meet with them—silently petition the Lord to work in your meetings together. And remember to thank Him as you watch Him work.

As you interact with people even before you know their language, pray prayers that sound like this: "Lord, give me the words, the countenance, and the expressions that will show You to her through me." Look for the ways He is answering and rest in His sovereignty. The Lord is at work through prayer.

LEARN

We must learn language and culture in order to do evangelism effectively. I wish I could say this process was easy for me, but truthfully, it was not. Thankfully, God used my efforts by His grace. While learning language, I immediately learned Scriptures

I could share. I did my best to learn a simple gospel presentation that I could begin sharing with my local friends. My language teacher did recordings of gospel presentations, and I put in the long hours of listening, repeating, and practicing. I used what I learned and trusted the Holy Spirit to bring understanding.

One of my language mentors gave me great advice: "Learn what you need and use what you learn." This helped me not be overwhelmed and to trust that God was developing my language in His timing. Even though my ultimate goal was more than recitations of rote gospel presentations, I needed to say what I could say when I could say it for two reasons. First, I wanted to develop the habits of sharing in the local language and to build those linguistic reflexes as soon as possible. Second, I wanted to share what I could share because I needed people to know that I followed Jesus. Taking the study of language and culture seriously is not a secondary part of your job. It is vital to take seriously in order to effectively communicate the most precious message on earth.

LISTEN

Every day I am more convinced that people communicate a lot more through what they don't say than through what they do say. This has pushed me to really invest in trying to understand others through praying for insight, listening deeply to their words, and by trying to take in as much of their situation as I can by way of intentional observation. This helps to overcome the natural tendency for people to express themselves verbally at a superficial level by noting that there is more being communicated than the words that are spoken. I noticed that when I listened well to what my friends were saying and followed up with good questions, they were more ready to share what was on their hearts.

For example, as my friend and I were walking through an incredible Central Asian park full of multicolored tulips, I asked her, "What is most important to you and your life?" In good Muslim fashion, she said, "Allah, my family, and my studies." I then asked, "Do these things bring you joy?" She did not immediately know the meaning of joy, so I explained how my relationship with God and following Him brought incredible joy. My listening carefully to her and asking good follow-up questions began to open up doors of further conversation about what meaning, life, and joy are truly about.

PROCLAIM

As I have noted already, sharing the gospel starts with prayer, it continues with understanding how to share the message in an understandable way and by using the local language, and it ends with a faithful proclamation of what God has done for the world through Christ. Depending on your context, this might need to start in different places in Scripture.

For example: In Muslim contexts, the definition of *sin* is very different than the Christian understanding. Therefore, faithful proclamation of the gospel does not often occur if you simply start with your testimony, transition to the Romans Road, and then issue a call to repentance. Faithful gospel proclamation in a Muslim context often requires the evangelist to begin in Genesis 1–3, explaining Who created the world, what went wrong, and what the consequences for sin look like from a biblical worldview.

If we are to proclaim the gospel as the solution to humanity's problem, we must first clarify the biblical perspective on what humanity's problem is. Ladies, this takes work. It is not easy to learn, it's
not easy to teach, but it is necessary to do to faithfully proclaim
the truth cross-culturally.

LIVE

God has taught me that my life tells a story. How I treat my
own coworkers, the clerk at the store, and people on the street
matters. God can use my character to raise questions about my
motivations that arise as my neighbors watch me and observe my
conduct. It is worth noting that even when this occurs, my neighbors have not yet heard the gospel; however, once they have heard
the gospel, what they observe can reinforce the truth and beauty
of the gospel as a life-transforming power.

Along with that He uses it to ready people's hearts for when
I get the chance to verbally proclaim the gospel to them. I found
that this can be as simple as buying cheese. At the bottom of our
apartment was a store that we frequented often. I noticed that
when I went to the cheese section at a certain time, I would find
the same employee working behind the counter. She was a student
at the local university. She went to school all morning, worked all
day, and studied most of the night. She was very kind, and if there
were no other customers, we often talked longer. I asked her questions about school, her family, her village.

One day she asked if we could meet outside of work so she
could practice her English. We met, chatted, and got to know
each other. Over time, she explained that she told her family all

about us. She told them that we were kind, always happy, and that we were different than other foreigners. Most important, she told them that we loved God and that seemed to be what drove us to these other characteristics.

We were most excited because my teammate and I had been praying that she would talk to her family about the things we had talked to her about! We were in a relationship with one precious student—a relationship begun due to my penchant for cheese—but through this relationship we saw the Lord take the stories, interactions, and impact of our lives to her family in a village. Daily I am reminded that living a life that displays Christ can lead to intentional proclamation. Live your lives, my dear sisters, in such a way that your actions match your verbal proclamation.

GOD ANSWERS

I sat in my house in Southeast Asia, fighting for faith and struggling to know how to live and proclaim the gospel in this new culture. By His Spirit, God directed me simply to step outside my house, walk down the street, and pray. I was nervous and cautious, but obedience got me out the door. I walked down the street, praying for all the things I saw. I prayed for houses and the families who lived within them. I prayed for the people who passed by me. As I walked through fields, I prayed for crops to flourish, for fisherman to catch fish, for the lady hanging up her clothes on the lines. I prayed for the leaders and the people I knew were in authority. I did my best to pray for everyone I saw. I prayed even that people would not think it odd that this light-skinned woman was living in a house by herself. And I prayed that they would talk to me.

My faith was so small, but I knew that God is big. He would answer in His perfect timing.

After months of these walks, a new coworker joined me in my city and became my roommate. One afternoon she and I walked onto our front porch and noticed that across the street a group of ladies were playing volleyball. I was stunned because, for three months, there had been little activity in my neighborhood. I was even more surprised when I noticed one of the women motioning to us, asking us to come join them.

For the next few hours, we played and communicated with the few sentences of the local language we had learned.

The next day as we went out for our "praying while walking" routine, something was different. Now the volleyball ladies stepped out of their homes to smile and wave at us. We got invited in for tea, and as we practiced our new language skills, our relationships began to form with these incredible local ladies. Until this point, our lives had consisted of praying, practicing the gospel in the local language with one another, and walking the neighborhood. Was God using this volleyball game to answer the prayers we had been petitioning Him for months?

I couldn't help but see these early relationships as part of the fruit of believing 1 Timothy 2:1–4. We had been petitioning God for everyone we saw for what seemed like fruitless weeks and months. And even though it felt like a long investment from our perspective, in God's good timing, He had used a simple volleyball game to open up avenues that would allow us to take part in the work He was doing in our neighborhood.

These neighborhood prayer walks, that led to a volleyball game, led to meeting my friend "Mary." Mary knew who I was because she would see me walk past her house regularly for months. God had been working on her heart as she watched these foreigners walk back and forth. God opened the door for me to speak the truth of the gospel to Mary. He gave us a close relationship, and God drew Mary's heart to Himself. It was not a quick process. We spent time together; we talked for hours about life and the Lord. We struggled through our differences of faith. We sang together as we did chores. All the while, I was trusting that my Father was at work as I prayed.

During the dailiness of life together, the Lord provided various opportunities to speak of the gospel. As she encountered the Word, God grew in Mary a heart that was drawn to the truth that she encountered in the pages of Scripture. She even started telling her friends and neighbors what God was doing. Through many answered prayers, through the hearing of the Word, and through the work of the Spirit, Mary's life changed for eternity. Mary went from a friend I met in Southeast Asia—one with whom I had little in common—to a sister with whom I will spend eternity. I do not have words to express how thankful I am that God would use my frail efforts to convey His glorious gospel to this dear sister.

Dear reader, as you are responding to your own call to go, I pray that you would feel the weight of your task. I also pray that you would know that you cannot succeed in this task by your own strength. In light of that, as you think of your work of evangelism, I want to plead with you to remember and believe God's Word as He says that our prayers as believers are effective. We are called to do the work of evangelism. That work involves praying, going, and proclaiming. It is a difficult task on so many fronts. But it is a task worthy of our efforts so that the nations can know the one true God who loves them. One day, we will stand alongside of our brothers and sisters from around the world, joyfully exhorting one another with the psalmist's praise shared on our lips: "Clap your hands, all you nations; shout to God with cries of joy. For the LORD Most High is awesome, the great King over all the earth" (Ps. 47:1–2 NIV).

CONCLUSION

As I close this chapter, I simply want to reiterate the charge to pray big prayers and expect God to work. Even when it looks like going out for yet another prayer walk through crowds of people whom you do not yet understand, He is working; He is preparing for Himself a spotless bride composed of the redeemed of the nations. He loves the people you will grow to love more than you ever could.

In the places where you do not yet understand, invest the time and energy to be a faithful and eager learner. Learn language and culture to the best of your ability and to the glory of God. Language learning is not a party trick to impress your friends when you are back home. It is the vehicle that you will use to carry the saving message of Jesus to the people who need to hear, repent, and believe. Take it seriously—as if your neighbor's eternity depends upon it.

And as you learn the language, commit to listening well. You have the privilege of entering into relationship with people and hearing their stories. One of the most important parts of cross-cultural communication is listening. Hear people's stories, listen to where God has been at work in their lives. Try to pick up on what they value, fear, hope for, and what embarrasses them. Connect these values and hopes with the truths that Scripture affirms and with the places it would challenge their cultural defaults.

Be patient yet bold with your friends as you trust the Lord to answer your prayers in His timing. As you share Scripture and proclaim the gospel, do it with confidence. It is true—and it is beautiful. Our God reigns as the holy and righteous King of the universe. Yet He also mercifully extends forgiveness to those who come to Him in repentant faith in Christ.

And in all things, live out the gospel that you are proclaiming. Let people see the life you are living match the gospel you are proclaiming. If you offend and need to repent, model the humility you are asking people to express before God. If someone offends against you, model the grace and mercy that you are telling them that God is ready to give to those who ask for it.

Reader, let us *go*, let us *go now*, let us *go tell* the gospel of Jesus Christ, because He "wants everyone to be saved and to come to the knowledge of the truth" (1 Tim. 2:4).

GUIDED PRAYER

God, we pray for the people to whom You are calling us. Thank You for the gift of being able to "go." As our feet hit the ground, would You place us among and around those whose hearts You are preparing to hear the gospel? Would You allow all circumstances in their lives to make their hearts tender to the good news of what You have done for them? We ask that You would allow our team to be the aroma of Christ where You place us. Thank You for Your sovereignty that orchestrates every detail for good and for Your glory. We trust You. Amen.

DISCUSS AND REFLECT

1. Do you have rhythms of praying for the gospel to reach the darkest places?

2. Who are you currently praying for that needs to hear the gospel?

3. What is holding you back from sharing Jesus with those He has put in your life and in your path right now?

4. Do you know someone in your church or community that together you can go out and share the gospel?

5. Is there any reason why you would not pray about going to the "ends of the earth" (Acts 1:8) to share the gospel of Jesus Christ?

CHAPTER 5

The Fellowship of Suffering

Ruth Ripken

From the General Editor

THERE ARE CERTAIN people in life whom God uses to disciple and train you through their close, life-on-life proximity. But there are also some whom you get to observe from afar who seem to have that same impact despite the distance. I can count on one hand the number of times I have interacted with Ruth in person; however, the life and testimony that she and her husband, Nik, have lived has had a profound impact on my family's life and walk with the Lord.

Before my husband and I went overseas, in my heart I quietly held the belief that since we were choosing something that looked different than the American dream, the Lord basically "owed us." We would do our part to give up a lot to go, but He would do His part to protect us from other hardship and trials. Now, I would have never verbally affirmed this belief, but it was something that I kept tucked away in the recesses of my heart that only the One who searches those places could see.

When a year into our time overseas the Lord allowed a season of intense personal suffering to enter our lives, it was the Spirit, the Word, and the testimonies of people like Nik and Ruth that held my heart steadfast. Their examples in suffering served to bolster and encourage me to trust in the goodness of our Father, even when life looked bleak and hopeless.

One gift that the Lord brought to me during this season of suffering on the field is how I saw that the Father intends to use everything—including my tears—to shape me into the image of the Son by the Spirit. How marvelous it is that we have a God who truly uses "all things [to] work together for the good of those who love [him and] are called according to his purpose" (Rom. 8:28). I learned some of this as He walked with me through this suffering, but I also learned much of it through listening to Ruth and Nik's stories. Their lives are a testimony to God's good work and purposes in the deepest, darkest moments of life. I am thrilled through this chapter to be able to invite you to let her wisdom encourage you to hold steadfast to the Father's plans and purpose.

THE FELLOWSHIP OF SUFFERING

As a child, I remember memorizing many of Paul's words about the love and grace of God. I recall with joy the words that were etched in my memory and on my heart about the way God brings the dead to life in Christ. I often found Paul's words to be among the most encouraging words that the Holy Spirit inspired in Scripture. Those life-giving verses stuck easily in my heart and flowed off my tongue on many occasions.

But one of the things that I had to learn to see—and which I learned all the more deeply through experience—was all that Paul has to say about suffering. In reality, when you begin to look for Paul's teaching on suffering, you notice how often he addresses it. The thing I began to see, though, is that where I instinctively tended to view suffering as something to avoid, Paul seems to see it from a different angle.

In his letter to the Philippians, Paul addresses suffering in multiple ways. In the first chapter, Paul tells the Philippians that his imprisonment, though it involves his own affliction, served the advance of the gospel among the prison guard. In chapter two, he famously calls his readers to take on the same mind as Christ who gave Himself up to serve the interests of those His sufferings would save. And in chapter three, Paul writes of his longing to know God and to know His fellowship—even amidst the anguish of suffering: "My goal is to know him and the power of his resurrection and the fellowship of his sufferings" (v. 10a). These were verses that sounded familiar, but which my heart had not deeply processed until the Lord walked me through sufferings of my own.

FINDING HIM FAITHFUL

When I think back to my early months on the mission field, one night stands out in my memory along with a whirlwind of vivid emotions. I recall lying on my back on a stretcher, looking up at the night sky in Malawi. I had kissed my precious husband goodbye, and two godly men were carrying me off to surgery. Despite the circumstances, I remember thinking about how the night sky above me was breathtaking. I had never seen the stars so bright. It seemed each one was bending down so I could see it more clearly.

I was nearly ten thousand miles from the familiar places that I had called home for thirty years, and the one familiar face of my husband was cut off from me as he was forced to wait outside of the operating room. Yet I distinctly remember that I did not feel alone. I had no earthly reason to feel the peace that embraced me as I looked into the night sky on my way to the surgeon. But still, my heart knew a deep sense of the sturdy and uninterrupted fellowship with my Creator who was with me. More than relief, I realized that it was the knowledge of that fellowship that I needed most at that moment. And it proved enough—more than enough.

The reason that I was on that stretcher that night was that my husband and I had not followed the single-most-repeated piece of advice we were given by those who had recently welcomed us to our new home in Africa: don't get pregnant during language school!

Now, typically, I am the ultimate rule follower. If they say don't walk on the grass, I don't. If they say don't cross the street except at the crosswalk, I'll walk an extra block to cross at the corner. Finding myself pregnant against the advice of our teammates and leadership didn't fit my personality. Now here I was, about six weeks into language school, dealing with morning sickness and the mixed emotions of "I disobeyed!" Of course, this was also mixed with the joyful excitement of adding an Africa-born child to our family. However, one morning I woke up with horrible cramps. Halfway through the day Nik and I left language school and headed to a doctor's office, where I was told that I was in the process of a miscarriage.

We were sent about an hour from the capital city to a village hospital, where two Christian doctors from South Africa met us upon our arrival. These two brothers in Christ used their expertise to help us medically, their presence to encourage us emotionally, and their sympathy to walk with us through the unexpected pain and grief.

We were not alone. As the medical staff circled my bed and prayed for the procedure, I sensed the fellowship of brothers and sisters in these strangers assuring me that I was not alone. Yet it was more than the kind staff or the men who carried me from the small hut to surgery that assuaged the sense of being alone. It was more than the knowledge that my dear husband would wait nearby through the long hours of the night that sustained me.

In that village hospital, I knew the fellowship of God in the midst of suffering in a way I had not yet experienced. I was going to need that fellowship over and over throughout the next thirty-five years we lived overseas. That night in the bush hospital began the baby steps in my journey to understanding what Paul was asking for in Philippians 3:10. But those were only the first steps on a road I am still walking.

Days after this first traumatic event in Africa, we experienced another blow. A phone call came to Nik, and on the other end of the line was his brother with some heart-wrenching news. At fifty-one years of age, Nik's mother had unexpectedly died of a heart attack. The healthy woman we had said tearful goodbyes to just a few months before was gone. We arranged for Nik to fly to America to be with his family and to participate in the funeral.

Lacking finances for all of us to return to the U.S., I stayed in Malawi with our two young boys. The Lord had provided a very caring community of workers always ready to help in Nik's absence. But it was something more—Someone more—that sustained me afresh as I grieved the loss of my pregnancy and my mother-in-law from a distance. I began to know what Paul meant when he made it his goal to know the fellowship of suffering.

REVISITING THE FELLOWSHIP OF SUFFERING

"My goal is to know him and the power of his resurrection and the fellowship of his sufferings . . ." (Phil. 3:10)

As we think about and even prepare for the loss, pain, grief, and suffering that may lie ahead of us on the mission field, it is helpful to reflect on the life of Paul we mentioned earlier. Paul is writing to the church in Philippi, expressing his love for this fellowship of believers while he himself is in prison. He had been instrumental in seeing many of them come to faith. He wants them to trust Jesus, to witness to the gospel, and to be ready to suffer. He wants them to know of the persecution he is experiencing, but also to glimpse the victory of Christ in which he is suffering confidently.

Paul promises them that what God started in these believers He will complete. Out of his suffering, he yearns for those he loves in the church he helped plant in Philippi to live in joy. He modeled for these believers how to have joy even in the midst of suffering. He wanted them to see him living out what he was calling them to.

In his letter to the Philippians, Paul insists that we rethink our relationship to suffering. It isn't about getting through suffering;

Jesus allows the suffering to bring us closer to the goal of a mature life with Christ.

According to Paul, it was through his suffering that he grasped the depth of Christ's love and power. It was through the toughest of days that he yearned to know Christ more. This came about through the tears of persecution. Paul saw fellowship with Christ as of supreme value through all of it. He threw off earthly wealth and status and recognized that crucifixion led to the resurrection. In Philippians 3:5–6, Paul gives us a list of all the education and accolades that had brought him pride and the feeling of accomplishment through his young life. Yet he also has come to see that these reasons to boast are nothing in comparison to the joy of knowing Christ (v. 8).

Paul knew he wasn't perfect. He struggled to pursue his goal of knowing Christ. He believed this would take place as he endured the suffering in order ultimately to reach that final goal. I can sense Paul gripping his pen even tighter as he writes how this will take place. He expects to discover the depth of the power of Christ's resurrection as he experiences the fellowship of His sufferings and, yes, even death.

Do we so yearn to see God's glory that we will welcome it if it comes wrapped in suffering? I know that I did not—and sometimes still do not—naturally seek to find the glory of God during suffering. Yet this seems to be a consistent theme throughout the New Testament.

FELLOWSHIP OF SUFFERING IN THE DEPTHS OF HEARTACHE

As strange as it may sound, Paul's words inviting us to share in the sufferings of Christ have become some of my most cherished verses. God has shown us the reality of the fellowship of His sufferings as He walked with me as I was left alone in Africa, grieving a miscarriage and the death of my mother-in-law. He proved Himself faithful later that year as we began dealing with chronic malaria that eventually forced us to move from Malawi and people we loved. And He proved Himself a faithful companion in even greater suffering that was yet to come.

Years later, I found myself standing in a hospital room in Kenya, with my oldest son by my side and my husband across the room next to the lifeless body of our sixteen-year-old son. As I alternated between weeping and feeling numb, the Holy Spirit used Philippians 3:10 to strengthen my buckling knees and to comfort my swirling mind. While my heart was going to crash through my chest and everything in my stomach was about to come up, this verse and God's faithfulness in the past sustained me.

After our son's death, we walked through six months where every day was a struggle. Getting out of bed, walking to the bathroom, cooking a meal, cleaning the house. It was a routine of taking one step at a time. I would sit in the chair where I did my morning devotions, open my Bible, and attempt to read. Each morning the tears poured out and all I could see through the blur was one word or verse, and I would cry out, "Help me, Jesus!"

Months later, Nik and I both came to the realization that we could stay in the pit of despair, or we could choose to find joy in the midst of the pain. We made a conscious decision to choose joy as we grieved. In doing so, we discovered afresh that we were not alone.

The Lord held me up—He held *us* up—by His ever-present fellowship in the depth of anguish and affliction. Even as the storm of every parent's worst fear crashed over us, I found fellowship with the One who walked suffering's road to victory before me. His victory assured me that a day is coming when He will lead me in triumphal procession into His eternal kingdom, where He Himself will wipe away every single one of these tears.

THE GLOBAL FELLOWSHIP OF SUFFERING

If you are reading this, I am guessing that you are personally considering being a part of God's frontline work among the nations. As you say yes, you will learn to eat foods that may be outside of your preferences. You will model for your children how to love the people and cultures that surround them—even when it is hard. You will have to wrestle with whether to send your children to a local school in a language you are just learning yourself or to homeschool them. Or you might even send them off to a boarding school. You will spend long hours trying to learn a local language, often sounding like a first grader.

In the middle of all of these sacrifices you are making to pursue your calling, you might find yourself tempted to think that God will put a special hedge of protection around you. You might assume that He will keep suffering at a distance in order to make "all things work together for the good of those who love God, who are called according to his purpose" (Rom. 8:28). But it is worth noting that the same person who penned those words in

Romans wrote about God's fellowship in suffering. Suffering and God working for our good may not be as mutually exclusive as we would like to think.

Over the past twenty years, Nik and I have had the weighty privilege of learning this lesson about the fellowship of suffering from the global church. We have been privileged to do research around the world, collecting the testimonies of brothers and sisters who have walked through persecution and suffering for the gospel. We have met some of our living heroes of the faith, and their stories have given fresh wind to our faith.

In this season of ministry, God has allowed us to visit and learn from hundreds of believers who live in places where it has cost them much to follow Christ. They have shared about their beatings, torture, imprisonment, isolation, and being ostracized from their families, villages, and communities. In this process, I have come to see ways that my sufferings join alongside these giants of the faith. Our shared, collective testimony is that God is always faithful. I am surrounded by a cloud of witnesses—biblical and contemporary—whose stories of suffering did not diminish the beauty of their fellowship with God. They—and I—have found this fellowship to be sturdy enough to sustain us even in the deepest pits of despair.

Before we close this chapter, then, I want to share with you a few pieces of advice that I have come to treasure for myself as a result of what the Lord has allowed me to learn about navigating seasons of suffering.

JOY IN THE FELLOWSHIP OF SUFFERING

As you prepare to head to the mission field, dear sister, I want to encourage you to cultivate an awareness of the fellowship that you share with God here and now in the gospel. I want you to do this today so that you are prepared to live in it tomorrow—no matter what suffering or success tomorrow may hold.

There is a part of me that wants to pray that the Lord would keep you from suffering, yet I have come to believe that this may not be the best way to pray or encourage those preparing for the Christian life. So instead of giving advice on avoiding suffering, let me offer some insights on how to see suffering as an opportunity for fellowship with the One who has already defeated suffering and death and who will hold you faithfully as you pass through the trials that lie ahead.

Don't Let Suffering Catch You Off Guard

Your ability to stay the course, to endure, to share in Christ's suffering begins before you arrive on the field. All too often, Western missionaries go to the field with a certain naivety about suffering. Because our pre-field lives are often conditioned to avoid suffering—or even to see it as punishment from God—we can arrive on the mission field unprepared to suffer well.

We have functionally put the kind of suffering faced by the apostles and the early church in the past tense. Only rarely do we hear about the contemporary suffering for the gospel experienced by our global brothers and sisters. It is not surprising, then, that when many missionaries face hardships related to leaving for

81

overseas or upon arriving on the field, they respond with doubt about their calling and many even quit prematurely.

My husband, Nik, has been faithfully reminding me for years that when we are faced with trials, we need to look forward and think about when the trial is over. *Would we be proud of the way we handled the difficulty set before us?* This question has caused me to reflect upon my actions in the midst of trials to try and gain a better perspective.

Beloved sister, I want to say this with all the weighty and sober clarity it deserves: Your ministry overseas may involve unbelievable pain, persecution, and suffering. The Lord may walk you through physical, emotional, spiritual, and psychological suffering beyond anything you have ever experienced. We must not expect that the followers of Jesus will avoid His suffering. He told us to expect it in His unchanging Word.

You may find yourself in a place where the suffering is something you see more than you suffer. You may walk by countless children with swollen bellies, old people with twisted bodies, and beggars on every street corner. This will indelibly change the way you look at the world and how you pray. But the hardest part of these heart-wrenching sights is that those without Christ are enduring this suffering without hope.

Do not lose sight of the fact that you bring eternal hope into the midst of the abject suffering that millions experience. Your heart will likely break in many ways as you see the wretched condition of people's lives. But do not let exposure to this kind of suffering cause you to shrink back from delivering the message of eternal rescue that those suffering need even more than clean

THE FELLOWSHIP OF SUFFERING

water or medical care. This is why we go—to bring hope today and eternally into the midst of hopeless suffering.

Choose to Cultivate Dependence

Throughout your life and ministry, the Evil One will attempt to drive you away from what the Lord is calling you to. Yet no matter what the Evil One throws at you, you must make the choice: Will you cling to the Lord where He has you or flee from the parts of His calling that are difficult?

Your commitment to clinging to Jesus in dependence is something you can begin cultivating even now. We received this advice through some of our interviews with persecuted believers in East Asia who had experienced years in prison as a result of their faith. Those believers shared with us their perspective on Christian growth in suffering, saying, "You can only grow in prison what you take into persecution with you." In other words, practice the disciplines today that you will need to get you through suffering. Just because you may not be experiencing suffering today does not mean that you need Jesus any less than you will when the Father shepherds you through the valleys. Just like getting on a plane will not make you an evangelist in another country if you weren't already sharing the gospel in your home country, going to prison will not make you faithful to cling to Jesus if that is not already your cultivated habit in freedom.

You are preparing for hard times today! The habit of clinging to Jesus in dependence will serve you well in times of relative ease and will be your ballast in the midst of desperation. Cultivate dependence today so that you have reflexes trained to respond in faith when trials arise.

Develop Habits of Leaning on the Body

God created us for community. All of us—even missionaries on the front lines of lostness—need community. No matter how strong we are, we need the help, gifts, and strength of the body of Christ to carry on in the midst of suffering. As Simon of Cyrene carried the cross of Jesus, we have the honor and joy of carrying our brothers and sisters in persecution who no longer can carry themselves. I believe that bearing each other's burdens is one of the most practical reasons that Jesus has for building His church.

Unfortunately, many new missionaries arrive on the field and join teams of missionaries who don't get along. Interpersonal tension can cause us to withdraw from those whom God has placed in our lives to assist and partner with us. Let me plead with you on this point: When you are tempted to disconnect from the body of believers because things are tense, don't do it! Don't withdraw from one another.

Just as lions chase their prey away from the herd and into vulnerable isolation, Satan loves to isolate us as he prepares to attack us. While stressful situations naturally provoke our fleshly tendencies to lash out at one another, we must recognize our more pressing need to lash ourselves to one another. In the midst of stress and suffering, we must continue worshiping together, eating together, and encouraging one another even when it may seem more natural to us to withdraw.

The thing is, not only do we need a loving, supportive Christian community for ourselves, but we also need to demonstrate what it looks like to those around us. In cultures of new believers who are in the process of shedding old ways, we must put on display how the bride of Christ responds to wrongs and hurt feelings. She imitates and extends the gracious forgiveness of Christ instead of allowing bitterness and jealousy to sow division.

As we develop habits of leaning on the body, we also teach new believers how to serve within the church. Missionaries can be reticent to receive the ministry of those they see won to Christ. But to refuse to receive the ministry of local believers is to rob them of opportunities to give sacrificially of their time and use of their gifts.

After the death of our son, I did not prepare a meal until we left the field three months later. Instead, the local body of believers took it upon themselves to feed us, sing over us, hold us, and love us. Our Kenyan church came each night with their praise team and sang us to sleep. As we cried and dealt with the pain and the suffering, the church body stood in our living room and interceded for us with prayer and song for eight straight nights. Our brothers and sisters would not allow us to fall and, at times, I can say that God used them to completely carry us. But we already had cultivated a sense of dependence upon these dear brothers and sisters prior to our disaster, so receiving their ministry was as natural as it was necessary.

Continue to Look Beyond Your Experience

It is important that, in suffering, we continue to look both upward and outward. Setting our attention on these two horizons is important because when we are walking through suffering, we often find ourselves most naturally turning inward toward our own pain and struggle.

After the death of our son, we knew we needed some counseling and time to listen to what God had next for us. However, after He had provided us with the gift of some time to heal, the Lord sent us on a global pilgrimage to learn from believers in persecution.

As we introduced ourselves to various brothers and sisters living in hard situations, we had the opportunity to share with them the experience of losing our son and some of the struggles the Lord had walked us through. In those moments together, God allowed our story to connect with the stories of suffering that these men, women, and families were experiencing themselves. We experienced a deep sense of bondedness at the point of shared suffering. Though each story was different, our stories all intersected at the point of sharing the fellowship of suffering and being sustained by God in the midst of it.

Listening to these dedicated and faithful giants of the faith also put what we had lived through in perspective. Hearing what God is doing in and through others helped us to see that we are a part of His faithful work around the globe, not isolated and alone in our suffering. While we should continue to grieve our own suffering well, recognizing the ways that God's faithfulness has sustained others of our brothers and sisters through their trials redirects our attention gratefully upward and sympathetically outward. This multi-horizon perspective can not only hasten our healing, but it can deepen our faith and extend our ministry.

STAY IN THE STORY

Finally, let me encourage you to trust the Lord with the story that He is writing for you instead of pining after someone else's story. In your flesh you will have ample opportunities to drift toward jealousy as you see the lives of your friends enjoying the familiarity of life back home or as you watch others enjoy more success in ministry than you are experiencing. The temptation to covet someone else's story will only be amplified in times of suffering when it looks like everything is better for everyone else. But let me encourage you to stay the course and let Jesus lead you where He will.

In those first few months in Malawi with a miscarriage, a death, and a job assignment change, it would have been really easy to quit and to jump out of where God was asking us to stay. But we didn't. We had planned from the beginning to be obedient to whatever God asked us to do. And everything within us said that God was leading us to stay.

This decision to stay in God's story for us did not mean that we never wished for a different narrative. There are some chapters of our story where the pages look wrinkled because of tearstains. There are some chapters I wish weren't there. There are some chapters that have left a mark on me that probably will always be there. But looking back, I am so glad He was faithful to hold us where He did. And looking ahead, I know that the final chapter leads to an unshakable kingdom and a trustworthy King. Do not look for shortcuts around the paths He leads you on—even when they are hard. Your calling is to walk closely with Him, neither running ahead nor falling behind. In the end, you will find that the peace you were after came from the One in whose presence you walked, not the condition of the path you followed.

I don't know all the reasons that God allows different types of suffering, and usually I cannot even offer a guess. There are times when God miraculously shakes the prison cell and releases people from prison like He did with Peter. There are times when the body that is praying for their friend's release gets to hear his knock at their door as an immediate answer to their prayers. Yet there are also those other times when the prisoners remain in prison, facing beating after beating.

There are ways that I know Christ now that I would have never understood without the sufferings we experienced. There have been victories and events that we would have missed if, when we were knocked down, we didn't get back up. There is a confidence that God will show up because we have seen Him do so in the past. Get up. Stay in His story for you until you see Him face-to-face and hear that "Well done."

Dear reader, I don't know what God has in store for you. What I do know is that you can trust Him with your days. He is a good, faithful, and merciful heavenly Father who will not waste anything. As you walk with God in the places He calls, you will walk through seasons of suffering, but you will not walk alone.

DISCUSS AND REFLECT

1. Think about the most difficult struggle or trial you have faced. Looking back now after the event, consider how you handled the situation. Were there things you wish you would have done

differently as you look back on your reaction, your words, your emotions?

2. Consider what would cause you to leave the field. Think through what your limits might be for you to stay in the story.

3. Review your definition of suffering. Is your definition one that is present, active, and includes you and your family?

CHAPTER 6

Married on Mission

Emily Watkins

From the General Editor

AMONG THE CONTRIBUTIONS to this book, this next chapter is unique. While in one sense it is about marriage, you are not going to find advice on how to keep your marriage strong on the field. Another book should be written on that. What you are going to find is something that both Emily and I have a great conviction about: in most situations, there is no such thing as a missionary spouse.

If you are married and are going overseas, God has called both of you. You are not an add-on to your husband, but you as a couple are being called together to put on display and proclaim the glory of God. Your husband will not reach 50 percent of the population. Women need to take up the task of reaching women.

Now, of course there are different seasons in life where what "work" looks like will be different. Sometimes ministry outside of the home will be more strategic and targeted because of responsibilities and ministry at home. However, I believe Emily provides us with a convicting testimony as to how the Lord changed her understanding of who she is in Him and what role the Father was asking her to play.

Another unique thing about this chapter is that I got to watch the work God did in her as a teammate. I got to see firsthand how Chris (her husband) did his best to push Emily to use her gifts and vice versa. Their marriage and ministry in and of itself was such a testimony on the field. I am praying that God would use her story both to convict and challenge you in your ideas of what role the Father would have for you *before you go.*

MARRIED ON MISSION: NOT A MISSIONARY SPOUSE

Chris and I met when I was in the eighth grade. We were friends, dated, got engaged, and got married by the age of twenty. Chris was an old soul from the beginning and had a five-year plan from the time I met him at age thirteen. In kindergarten he said he wanted to be a missionary. When he was sixteen, he committed to go into full-time ministry. By the time we entered college, he was already considering full-time missions.

At this point in my walk with the Lord, I was fine with Chris talking about going into ministry. I thought it was wonderful! But full-time missions? Short-term trips here and there were fine. Full-time missions work was another story. Even despite my limited understanding at that time, I knew that the life of a missionary would be significantly different than a life with my husband as a pastor. At that point in my life, a comfortable home, steady jobs, and two to three kids seemed pretty appealing.

After much prayer, we really felt like we needed time apart to seek out where the Lord was leading us. If we were going to get married, I wanted to *want* to do missions. But at that point, I very much did not. Chris was scheduled to go on a mid-term trip to India the summer before my freshman year in college, and so, in an effort to figure out my own calling, I joined a separate trip to Burkina Faso. If I am honest, my real expectations for the trip were to see some cool places, get some good stories, share the gospel with some villages, and help people with physical needs. My plan was then to return, tell Chris that the experience had not changed my perspective much, and that I was not sure we should consider going long-term if we were going to get married.

Praise God that He can take the most skeptical and cynical heart and bring transformative change. Burkina Faso *was* cool. I definitely had some crazy stories, and we did get to share the gospel in some villages. But God did way more than just that. During my time in Burkina, God placed the question in my heart: "Do I, Emily—separate and distinct from Chris—truly believe the gospel message and all of its implications?" The Lord moved to call me to the nations and see that there were so many souls, so many women, who did not know about Jesus.

As hard as I knew it would be to shift my vision of what my life would look like, I could not ignore this calling that the Lord had placed on my heart through this trip. Similarly, Chris also came back from India with his sense of a call to full-time missions confirmed. We got engaged, got married, and Chris enrolled in a seminary program that required two years overseas as a part of the requirements for completing the degree. We were set to go.

However, in my heart of hearts, I still expected Chris would do the heavy lifting in terms of active ministry on the field. He, of course, was the one with the seminary training. And so, in my mind I did not think much of my role in missions aside from being willing to go. In my mind, he would be the active missionary for our family, and I would support. So, after a few years of training, we set off for the Middle East—Chris with his seminary degree, and I intending to contently follow.

Yet, God gave me opportunity after opportunity in pregnancy centers and with women to serve in ways that Chris couldn't. I thought Chris would do the bulk of the work—until God began to reveal that my calling to take up His cross and follow Him was one of service too. I couldn't experience Him or serve Him vicariously through Chris. I was called to do that myself. He called me to ministry. He called me to go to the nations. I was not to be a missionary wife. I was to be a missionary!

As the Lord began to show me this, I realized my life was being driven much more by what I deemed to be Chris's calling, not on what the implications of being saved by grace were for me. I was not focusing on the fact that I was a sinner saved and redeemed by Jesus on the cross, and that the Great Commission was for me as an individual follower of Jesus. The Lord began to show me that because of the gospel, I was individually called to participate in the kingdom work. What the Lord stirred in me in Burkina was specifically for *me*. He called *me* to ministry. He called *me* to go to the nations. I was not to be a missionary wife. I was to be a missionary! In fact, I have come to wonder if we should simply do away with the idea of a "missionary spouse" altogether.

These musings are not just prompted by my experience, however. They are grounded in some passages of Scripture that have come to shape and reshape my understanding of the calling to ministry as something more native to my nature as an image-bearer. In the following section I want to briefly suggest a few passages of Scripture that should cause us to reconsider our ideas about what it means when God calls a married couple to the mission field. Each of these passages provides way more material than I can unpack in the space allotted, but I pray that what I do have space for can prompt some reflections in you as you consider your role in missions.

THE INDIVIDUAL CALL TO REFLECT CHRIST

One of the key concepts that the Lord used to teach me about my role as a follower of Jesus, distinct from Chris's role, was the concept of being an image-bearer. As a mom of three young children, I've had the privilege of watching *The Lion King* so . . . so . . . so . . . many times. While *The Lion King* is not exactly an accurate depiction of the gospel, I often think of the scene where Rafiki tells Simba his father is alive and takes Simba to the pond. He tells Simba to look in the pond, but Simba says, "That's not my father; that's just my reflection." Rafiki pushes Simba, "No, look harder. You see, he lives in you." Simba sees his reflection become the image of his father. Inspired after seeing his father and remembering who he is, he then returns courageously to lead the pride as Mufasa would have done. One could say that he returns with this reminder of his identity to bear the image of Mufasa to the rest of his kingdom.

Clearly there are breakdowns in this metaphor, but it is a basic picture that I have used to talk to my kids about being an image-bearer. This idea of being an image-bearer altered how I thought about my calling in this life as a follower of Jesus, which drastically affected my calling and ministry on the mission field.

In Genesis 1:26 (NIV), the Lord says, "Let us make mankind in our image, in our likeness." Verse 27 (NIV) goes on to say, "So God created mankind in his own image, in the image of God he created them; male and female he created them." I knew this simple verse as a kid, but the more time that I spent overseas, the more I realized I had memorized but not truly internalized and processed this verse.

What does it mean to be created in the image of God? John Piper, when speaking about being made in the image of God, said:

> In salvation, two things happen. The mirror gets turned around, and we see the glory of God again, and the defilement that had gone over the face of it gets wiped off gradually, and we begin to reflect God. So, I think being created in the image of God means that we image God. We reflect God. We live in a way, we think in a way, we feel in a way, we speak in a way that calls attention to the brightness and the glory of God.[7]

Not only were male and female created as image-bearers in Genesis, but we see in Scripture that we are being restored to the image of Christ when we receive the gospel (Rom. 8:29). As we are restored to His image, we are also commissioned to bear it before the watching world. Therefore, by faith in what Jesus has done for me, I am personally and individually transformed and called to bear testimony to my image-restoring Lord.

You see, as I began seeing Christ more clearly, I have also come to see that I am individually both privileged and responsible to reflect Him. While the details of the life I share with my husband may affect the *hows* and *wheres* of our shared calling to bear Christ's image, my individual responsibility and calling cannot be satisfied by what my husband does in fulfilling his calling. I am supposed to reflect Christ where He calls me. I do not do that simply by standing behind my husband, hoping he's reflecting Him for us both.

GOSPEL GRATITUDE AND INDIVIDUAL RESPONSIBILITY

Friend, can I encourage you right now to put down this book, look to the Father, and thank Him for His goodness? Thank Him for not only making you in His precious image, but also for His costly work of restoring the image of Christ in you. And then, as you do so, consider the audacious privilege that it is for you to be an image-bearing ambassador of His gracious gospel to the rest of the world! Cultivating fresh gratitude for the privilege of bearing Christ's image will affect how you approach your calling to bear witness.

Early on in my journey with the Lord, I was getting the order of identity and occupation mixed up. I was more focused on the task of going to the mission field rather than the reason behind the task. I was trying to obey Christ dutifully without basking in the wonder of what Christ had done for me. This made it easy to think that I was just along for the ride. I was being obedient, dutiful, and supportive—but I was not caught up in the beautiful, weighty privilege of the mission for myself.

If we fail to consistently look to Christ in our calling, we will fail to reflect His image as we must. That is how I could feel content to simply see Chris as the primary missionary with myself as the missionary spouse. I had lost sight of my motivation for mission work in the first place. If we fix our eyes on Christ, the overflow of our gratitude-infused awe of being made—and remade—in His image will naturally push us into active kingdom work.

So, married women, learning from my past, let me challenge you to evaluate: Are you personally bearing God's image—and the ambassadorial call that comes with it—to the nations? And similarly, is your spouse also individually bearing God's image to the nations? Marriage is a beautiful union of two followers of Christ, partnering together in the gospel. This is an amazing gift, but the gospel message is individual and personal so we both have callings that entail both privileges and responsibilities. Our relationship with Christ is not mediated through our spouse. Our relationship is directly with the King of kings. We encounter Him and He uses that encounter to shape how we reflect Him. Married women, remember that you have encountered the Father personally and your call to reflect Him comes directly from seeing Jesus. How you reflect Christ will be distinct from how your spouse reflects Christ.

MAKING SPACE FOR EACH OTHER'S MINISTRY

One way we can display this is when we, as spouses, care for one another. The husband's call is to love his wife as Christ loved the church and gave Himself up for her. The wife is likewise to submit and respect her husband. Christ loves the church, and the church loves Christ—both displaying selfless, sacrificial love. But because our primary identity is children of God who have been individually saved and redeemed by the blood of the Lamb, who each have the calling of the Great Commission, the goal of loving each other in marriage should be wanting the other spouse to pursue the Lord and His distinct calling on their life.

In reflecting on this, I have come to ask: "How can I work to support Chris's walk with the Father? How can I help encourage him into the ministry to which the Father has called him in this season?" Likewise, Chris's questions are: "How can I work to support Emily's walk with the Father? How can I help encourage her into the ministry to which the Father has called her in this season?" Once you have answered those questions, the work of making room in your schedules and rhythms to free each other to do the things to which you are called will take intentionality, but it will bear fruit in ministry and in the observed love and consideration you share for each other.

If this is not a part of how you and your spouse think about your marriage, I would beg you consider these questions. First, ask yourselves the question: "What am I clinging to as my primary identity?" Is it in being a missionary? Is it in being a wife? Or a mom? Or is it in being a child of God? Second, ask yourself the question: "In our marriage, are we supporting each other in our relationship with the Lord and in the different ministries the Lord has given us?" Pray for the grace and ability to do this in your marriage.

When you're serving on the field, work to discover how each of you can be active in ministry, whatever that may look like for your family. If you are working in a place that lacks gospel access, it is not just the men of that population who lack this access. And in almost every one of these situations, it would be unwise—culturally and practically—for a man to attempt to disciple women. Women must be engaged in that frontline work of sharing the gospel and discipling women.

This may look different for you and your spouse, but you are both called to participate in kingdom work. When you and your spouse serve and equip each other, this does not go unnoticed by the people you live and work among. This intentional and sacrificial love that can be displayed in marriage is one of the best bridges to talk about Christ and how Christ was the first to provide this example.

DIFFERENT MINISTRIES AND MARRIAGES

Having written this much, I want to stop and acknowledge that where I started in my journey toward the field may not parallel your story. Maybe you and your husband are both aligned in your calling and what that may look like overseas. Or maybe you are the one who is fiercely wanting to go to the mission field and who has the plan to be intensely engaged in active ministry. Maybe you both have trepidation about what the Lord is calling you to. Whatever your marriage situation, one thing that I do know applies to every believer living in this broken world: it is extraordinarily easy to forget our individual calling as followers of Jesus, first and foremost.

We often get distracted and our driving force in life easily shifts. Good things, honorable things—things like marriage, friendships, work, parenthood, and even service—can become primary. We are tempted to put good things before Christ. Ministry without rootedness in the gospel is not kingdom work. It might be great service, but when anything comes before our calling as followers of Christ and being image-bearers of Him, we will begin to mission-drift.

DIFFERENT GIFTS, DIFFERENT SEASONS, BUT THE SAME CALLING

Throughout this chapter I have really just been arguing for one thought: *all women can and should be used by God to be a part of the kingdom work.* What I need to make sure to clarify here at the end, however, is that every woman, every ministry, and every family will be different in how that kingdom work plays out. We also have to acknowledge that there are different seasons of life and ministry, so kingdom work may change during different times in our lives.

Some women will serve through leading the team. Some women will minister in developing strategy. Others will find opportunities to connect directly with the people they are serving through their kids and connecting with other moms. Some women will find their place in the marketplace and engaging employees, while others will find a niche in studying and helping facilitate language learning. Sometimes your kingdom work is intentionally within the walls of your home and sometimes there are opportunities in local churches to lead other women.

During various seasons throughout the years I spent on the field, I engaged women from our people group directly, worked with strategy at another time, and in another season was primarily and intentionally at home with one of my children full-time. Ministry changes and the Lord's providence is always beyond our understanding. Be open to the Lord's guidance in how He wants to use you overseas, even if it is not how you expect. The Lord's plans are often not our plans. But whatever your season or the tasks that the Lord places in front of you, make sure that you are doing them as one called to these tasks in service of King Jesus.

Many of you will be going to join teams of other missionaries. If you do find yourself serving on a larger team, it can be tempting to shrink back and fade into the background. But sister, hear me clearly: your perspective is extremely valuable, and your calling is sure. Don't shrink back—lean in and play your role. Your team needs you, and you need to fulfill your ministry calling. Consider the often-repeated image of the church as a body and the implications for each part being necessary in the work of the whole (1 Cor. 12:12–31; Rom. 12:3–6; Eph. 4:1–16).

Also, remember it is okay for your marriage and work to look different than the next family. The Lord gifts His children differently. Support and encourage those differences rather than all trying to be the same. Affirm other married women in how the Lord has gifted them rather than compare. Spur each other on in the calling to be image-bearers, whatever that may look like. God has made you unique to do His work in a certain way. Rarely is that the exact same as your teammate or friend. Remember who you are accountable to and follow His leading.

MY PRAYER FOR YOU

To all the married women who are reading, know that your marriage will be tested and tried throughout your time on the field. Remember that, above all things, love God and love each other. If you take nothing else from this chapter, my advice is for both you and your spouse to ensure you cling to the Father and prioritize Him as individuals and in your marriage. Remember when Jesus was with Mary and Martha. Martha was busy doing tasks to care for Jesus, while Mary was sitting at Jesus's feet (Luke 10:38-42). One thing is necessary: work to prioritize abiding with the Father above all.

The gospel message and the love of the Father are the fountain from which all kingdom work comes, including your relationship with your spouse. When culture shock hits, care for each other well. When suffering hits, know the Enemy causes divisions and be on your guard for this in your marriage. When you are depleted and hitting those lows, or even when you are hitting those highs, care for each other and make sure your spouse has time to commune with the Father and do active ministry, whatever that is. Think and pray together as a couple about how you can care for each other before going to the mission field. These patterns stick with you and can work to grow your care for each other on the field. Chris and I still intentionally try to reserve time each day for the other person to read, pray, and rest, and that began when we were overseas.

Remember, sister, the gospel that you are going to proclaim to the nations is the same gospel that allows any marriage to function and enables broken people to love and care for one another—grace given because the ultimate grace has been received. Remember that both you and your spouse have been redeemed by the Father, and you both have incredible work before you!

DISCUSS AND REFLECT

1. Am I going overseas because of my understanding of the gospel?

2. Am I relying on my spouse's calling rather than my own? Is my spouse relying on my calling?

3. Are there differences in how we feel called to missions? What are those differences?

4. How are you as a married couple expecting to reflect Christ together and individually?

5. What are some ways that my husband and I can love each other by supporting each other in our kingdom work on the field?

CHAPTER 7

Going Single

Sydney Dixon

From the General Editor

My FIRST MEMORY of Sydney was sitting next to her during a philosophy class early in our seminary careers. She was one of those girls who you know—from the moment you meet her—that she loves Jesus. Her kindness and contentment in Christ were something you could sense even just by sitting next to her. She was also crazy smart.

I remember as our professor passed back our tests, my head fell to the table in relief. I got a C. I passed! I was thrilled! But then I looked over and noticed an A scrawled across the top of Sydney's paper. She had to have been the only A in the entire class. Jealousy surged in me, but after making a joke about it with her, her humble acceptance of success and contagious joy were so real, I couldn't help but try and be her friend. Maybe she would even let me study with her.

God has done much with Sydney's life since those days in philosophy class. She has worked with Cru (formerly Campus

Crusade for Christ) for ten years in Eastern Europe and Russia, serving in many different capacities both Stateside and abroad. She is currently in her eighth year serving with the International Mission Board in Southeast Asia, and she is also working on her PhD in applied theology. Sydney has an incredible resume; however, should you meet her, please poke fun at her unashamed love for cats, which may be her only personal flaw.

My admiration for Sydney started with her intellect and has since grown in even greater degrees as I have watched her follow Jesus wherever He has called her. I have observed from afar as God has asked very difficult things of my friend, and repeatedly she has said with her words and actions that He is worth it. I pray as you read her words that you would be encouraged by her example to follow Jesus no matter what stage of life you are in.

GOING SINGLE

Have you ever told God no? I did. In fact, I remember the occasion quite vividly. It was my senior year of college while driving to campus, and I was so ready to be finished with studies.

I loved university life, but I was ready for the next thing. The previous summer I had spent six crazy weeks in Eastern Europe. Although it was filled with squatty potties and mice, it was also an amazing summer filled with opportunities to share Jesus with people who didn't even believe God was real. By the end of that summer, I had said yes to return to serve God through a one-year internship in college ministry. But this day—on my drive to campus—God pushed it too far. I felt an overwhelming sense that

God was asking me if I was willing to *go wherever, for however long.* My answer then was a fast and hard no.

This rapid reaction took me a bit by surprise. During university, my faith in God and my relationship with Him grew infinitely. It was as if the faith my family had instilled in me truly took flight and carried me along to greater heights of insight into the Scriptures and to greater depths of intentionally living my faith. God was definitely the most important person in my life, and walking in obedience to Him was my life's goal. Or, at least, I thought it was until that moment in the car when I so quickly responded to God in the negative. How did I dare just say no to God?

Over the days that followed I did some soul-searching. What caused me to say no to giving God everything? In His great kindness, God unearthed parts of me that I was unwilling to surrender for the long run. In my mind, it was perfectly reasonable to put my big life plans on hold for a year or two and follow the adventures God had in store. But if I agreed to go *wherever, for however long,* how was the vision I had laid out for my life going to come to fruition? You see, I desperately wanted to be a wife and mother. That had always been my dream, and it was not okay with me to consider postponing that indefinitely.

It's not like I lacked great examples of single people serving the Lord. We don't even have to look beyond the Scriptures for examples of men and women successfully (and seemingly with joy) serving God as singles. Paul—arguably the greatest missionary— was single. I mean, Jesus never married or had children! The Bible even speaks frankly to the advantages singles have in a pursuit of ministry. It is true that singles are freer to devote themselves to the work of ministry since they do not hold responsibility to care for a spouse and children (Matt. 19:10–11; 1 Cor. 7). Paul goes so far as describing singleness as a gift from God (1 Cor. 7:7). Can you imagine?! As true as these advantages are, none of them helped transform my no into a yes nor sustained me in the single life for many more years than I ever imagined would be. So then, the question remains: As a single woman having now lived on the field for more than thirteen years, what did transform my no into a yes? What truths of God have sustained me?

The road—from that day driving in the car to campus until now—has been long and sometimes very difficult, and it is one I have traveled as a single woman. I finally gave a reluctant okay to God's question regarding my willingness to go indefinitely to the places He would lead me. Amazingly, God took my tiny okay and quickly exploded it into a yes . . . even a yes, now please! But saying yes to God and not now to my own plans and dreams for a husband and family did not automatically prepare my heart for the possibility of that dream never actualizing. Obviously, my life's journey isn't over yet, and I have no idea if God will resurrect my old dream for a husband and family. But one truth about God's character to which I cling is His faithfulness (Ps. 89:8). This truth of God's character has enveloped me as I continue to say yes to Him each day, and it has enabled me to persevere—and often thrive—in this life.

ONLY LOVE

Time and time again, God has proven His love for me in His great faithfulness. My confidence in His unfailing love for me is the ground of my trust in Him through all circumstances. No matter our marital situation, as followers of Jesus, our devotion to Him is key. But if we are honest, sometimes saying yes to God is not enough to recognize God's faithfulness to sustain us through difficulties. This reality settled heavily upon me one freezing, dark, winter day in the early years of my life overseas. Just six months into my Eastern European life, I found myself greatly struggling with singleness and my place in ministry. Life in general was just hard. As I sat staring out the window, the landscape of the snow before me was blurred by tears while my vision of the future was warped by frustration and loneliness. I remember crying out to the Lord, begging Him to help me remain faithfully obedient to the life He had called me to live. In that moment, He brought loving correction to the ways I had allowed obedience to Him to supplant love for Him as first place in my life. This correction came through the words of His Son.

Matthew's Gospel records an exchange between Jesus and the religious leaders of His day. In one of their many attempts to catch Jesus in the wrong they asked, "Teacher, which command in the law is the greatest?" (Matt. 22:36). Jesus's response is simple yet profound, short yet thorough. He said, "Love the Lord your God with all your heart, with all your soul, and with all your mind. This is the greatest and most important command. The second is like it: Love your neighbor as yourself" (vv. 37–39). Through His gentle correction, God demonstrated His faithfulness to apply the truth of His word to the specifics of my life. I felt inadequate in ministry, but He faithfully redirected my heart back to the greatest responsibility—to love Him fully. I felt ill-equipped for life among seemingly hard hearts, but He faithfully reminded me that the sure path to loving others well is to seek Him first. I felt lonely, but He faithfully demonstrated He was with me. The course of my life once again changed through God's faithful expression of His character and loving devotion to me.

I realized that my passion to take the gospel to those who had never heard could (and did) turn frigid like the harsh Eastern European winter from the coldness of no apparent fruit in ministry. In truth, it was my obedience to His call to go that had been carrying me forward for some time. But the struggle to remain obedient in the lonely and agonizing moments of life was breaking me. It was clear that obedience alone would not sustain me. Only love for God would carry me through to a faithful walk of obedience in this life. Only a deep and abiding love for God would help me to love others, to walk in a lifetime of obedience to Him, and to rekindle my passion for the ministry. I was struck by the truth that love for God is paramount for a life well-lived with the Lord, whether I remained single or not.

REAL LIFE IN THE WHEREVER

God, out of His great love, had once again filled my heart with deep love for Him through His Word. I think it was an even deeper love than I had ever known before. Love for God has helped sustain me through many years of ministry. Love for God has helped me surrender a pursuit for the fulfillment of the dream to marry and have kids. All of life is truly, at its core, only about the love of God. Our faithful and loving God likes to give gifts to help us along the journey, and some of them are surprising. Allow me to share a few gifts of insight He has given me as I've traversed this journey as a single woman.

My Non-DNA Family

None of us gets to choose the family we are born into. Some are blessed with an amazing biological family (as I am!), and some of us, not so much. All of us who choose to move our lives abroad leave a majority (or all) of our family behind. But family is important. It is, after all, one of the key biblical word pictures for the church. However, even though our family remains in our passport country, it doesn't mean that we are destined to live without family around us. It is into this void that our non-DNA family (as a dear friend calls it) steps.

There are many ways to create a non-DNA family. For me, this family overseas has developed out of my teams, other expats, and national friends. But don't mistake any of these avenues to family as easy. Family is still family, and any family gets messy at times. Before you go, pray for the Lord to begin to prepare you and your non-DNA family members for one another. Then begin to cultivate the relationships God provides and watch them blossom into family.

Let yourself be amazed by how God will provide family out of the diverse groups of people in your life. Some of my dearest family have come out of ministry relationships with national friends. Not only have these relationships helped me walk through some of the loneliest days overseas, but my experience of life has been immeasurably enriched. I am better as a Christian, as a missionary, and simply as a human because of things I've learned through my non-DNA family.

As I reflect on more than thirteen years of living abroad, I am humbled by some of the ways in which God has constructed and used my non-DNA family of nationals. These deep, enduring ties of trust and commitment have allowed me privileged access into the hearts of people in cultures very different from my own that are often difficult to understand as an outsider. As a single female living far from "home," my national families have all but legally adopted me. The opportunity to be so fully enveloped into a local family has granted unique access to "real life" that has benefited my communication efforts in ministry beyond measure. I recently asked two of my national sisters why they think our family relationship has developed. They immediately responded that time spent together, mutually sharing deep issues of life in vulnerable honesty, has bound us together. The time afforded me as a single has been key to unlocking the inner door of family life and has allowed me to move from observing to participating deeply in the dynamics of family life within my "adopted" families. To be so loved and cherished by local families is a true gift from my faithful, loving God.

Realize That the Struggle Is Real

The struggles of life abroad are real—sometimes intensely real—and differ according to personal circumstances. No matter our situation, it is important to be honest about our struggles. The perfect missionary—whose ministry game is at 100 percent every single moment—does not exist. And if you think you've found the "perfect missionary," one of you is lying. The struggle for all lifers abroad is very real.

My "solo" life trek across the globe has brought seasons of great struggle and mourning. Doing real life in a different culture—particularly one that is not kind to females—is often not very fun as a single lady. When you are serving deep within a sea of people who don't love Jesus, the possibility of a life ministry partner (a husband) seems quite outside of the realm of possibilities. And if you commit your life to such a location, it can seem like your dream of ever having a husband is dead (or at least dying as each year passes). The loss of any dream is sad, and it's okay to mourn. The truth is that none of us knows fully the plans God set beforehand for us while we remain on this earth. What we do know is that He calls us to love Him first and fully, and He will give us the grace and peace to walk that path.

In those moments when the mourning of a dream seems all too real, it is important to have your Christian family as support. Seek out healthy relationships in which you can honestly share your struggles. Then rely on the Lord to work in your life and through the lives of your family to guide you through the dark days. And embrace the lighter days when the struggle is less intense. But remember you will never be that "perfect missionary." She doesn't exist.

Be Aware of the Need to Beware

In the thick darkness of difficult ministry, our solo situation can feel very isolating. And when we are not obligated to share every piece of our life with another human, we can dive deeply into isolation. Don't do it. Isolation is a dangerous place and ripe for opportunities for our Enemy. Be aware of personal tendencies and temptations. Be aware of how those may be magnified in your life abroad.

Living in a constant state of high stress (which even in its best moments typifies life lived cross-culturally) serves to intensify elements of our personalities and natural responses to our surroundings. For example, if you already struggle with a temper, then the refusal of the man at the market to sell you a hammer just because you are a girl and that's not your job will most likely lead to a rapid rise in the "temperature" of your response. (Not that I speak from personal experience on this!) Any type of previous trauma or addiction may serve as fertile ground for a renewed struggle. Can God give us victory over sinful inclinations? Absolutely. Just be aware that the typical experience of many Christians is a progressive struggle toward victory by the power of God's Spirit in our lives.

We live in a very sexualized, global culture. Unfortunately, the number of women struggling with classic forms of pornography is steadily on the rise.[8] We must be aware not only of sexualized temptations but also of unhealthy emotional temptations. Typical outlets for emotional romance fantasy include rom-coms and romance novels. I am not suggesting these escapes are all bad because we all need a light-hearted laugh every now and then; my caution is that these emotional outlets can be a catalyst for inappropriate dreaming.

Put in place regular check-ins with an accountability partner, preferably one who knows you well and with whom you will be honest. Someone who has lived or is living life abroad can be especially helpful, as they may have a clearer understanding of potential struggles for singles overseas.

Love Your Brother as a Brother

The uniqueness of the single-lady life overseas offers both delightful and challenging situations. One aspect of this life that is equal parts blessing and difficulty is the reality of needing our brothers. In an age of #MeToo and greater awareness of the extreme difficulties women face across the globe, I realize that stating the necessity of men in our lives may be unpopular. Nonetheless, it is true. Figuring out how to do this life as an army of women, sans men, is an understandable reaction to many of the difficulties women face. Girl power, right? Well, yes and no.

Gender segregation and discrimination are stark realities in an overwhelming majority of places with the greatest absences of gospel witness. Married couples and families offer these cultures a beautiful example of Christ-like familial relationship. But the incorporation of singles—functioning as sisters and aunts—into families expands the beautiful witness of Christian community to the surrounding society. You, as a single lady who loves Jesus and loves her Christian family (including the brothers), provide a unique example and broaden the picture of an often misunderstood and mistreated segment of the global community.

Beyond the healthy example of Christian family interaction that your diverse non-DNA family provides to the surrounding culture, there exist practical and emotional benefits to building brother-sister trust. Quite simply, in cultures that more readily ascribe dignity and respect to men, your brothers can provide a healthy platform for their Christian sisters to be recognized and honored as equally important human beings. For example, through the years, various brothers on my teams have helped make introductions on my behalf in communities (and churches), then appropriately deferred to me in discussions of strategy and their implementation. Unfortunately, without their intentional support, my ministry can become greatly hindered.

As an independent Western woman, the need to be introduced and validated in the eyes of any person or community by a man is extremely frustrating. Sadly, this is not the weightiest problem we face as women. Living in a culture where interactions with men can more commonly be fraught with some level of danger, remembering the Christlike love of my brothers brings healing. They provide a safe place to relate to men and help me combat the hardness of heart and resentment against men that can build within me in such an unfriendly environment. The hardship of being a female in my currently adopted culture is difficult. I have learned a tremendous amount from my local sisters about how to live with grace under such strain. But there are moments when it feels too much to bear. It is in these moments that a special thankfulness for my brothers arises. Receiving and witnessing Christ-honoring, healthy affection between brothers and sisters in Christ has offered a path to healing my own heart and frustrations that the culture can bring. In the absence of a husband—and with my father and own brother on the other side of the world—the sibling affection these brothers provide breathes a healing breath into my single life.

Is there cause for caution within cross-gender relationships among those who are not married to each other? Yes, and a multitude of resources has been produced emphasizing helpful precautions for interactions between men and women who are not married to one another. But the real need for caution does not negate the very real need for relationship. Men and

116

women—working as brothers and sisters—bring great benefit to one another's lives. So, love your Christian brothers well and express your desire to receive your brothers' appropriate and God-honoring love as their sister.

One final piece of advice from your big sister: Have fun and enjoy the amazing experience that is life overseas. Embrace the freedoms and flexibility being single uniquely affords you in ministry and also in the rest of your life.

PLEASE LORD, LET THAT NOT BE ME

When I finally embraced God's call for me to go *wherever, for however long* He may determine, I was quickly anxious to go. But just as my passion for ministry cooled in the harsh Eastern European winter, so, too, has my passion for the adventure waxed and waned. Two years or so into my life overseas, I found myself in a massive auditorium filled with women in my organization who had also committed themselves to full-time, vocational ministry. I don't recall much about that particular women's event. What I do remember is a panel of diversified women sharing their individual experiences and offering hard-won advice to their sisters in the work (much like the contributors to this book). On the panel sat a variety of women in different stages of life and ministry—a veteran empty-nester, a mom of young kids, a married lady with no children, and a single woman. To be honest, I cannot recollect any details about that single sister other than the fact that she was somewhere in her forties. However, a very distinct memory comes to mind of sitting in the audience and desperately crying out in my heart, "Please Lord, let that not be me."

Jump ahead with me to the present. As I sit here in a café, sipping my coffee and typing my thoughts to you many years later, the truth is that I have become that dear sister. The setting is different; we are conversing through words on a page rather than via a mic on a stage. But nonetheless, here we sit, as a panel of women who have gone before you. And here I am representing the experience of single women on the field. I promise you that now I truly count it an honor that the Lord has allowed that to be me, that I have the privilege to share with you a few pieces of my solo journey with the Lord. And I will continue to press into the love God has given me as I walk with Him in loving obedience *wherever, for however long* He allows.

Though my experience is not an exact road map for yours, perhaps pieces of it will be reflected in your coming adventure. God has greatly reshaped my dream for a husband and family through the years. For some of you, similar dreams may be postponed for a season. For some of you, it may be a very long season. But remember that the length of any season is appropriately set by God in His infinite wisdom, faithfulness, and love.

So I challenge you to love the Lord your God with all that you are and answer yes to go *wherever, for however long*, as long as it is with Him.

DISCUSS AND REFLECT

1. Are you willing to say yes to serving God wherever He may ask you to go, for however long He may ask you to go? If yes, what are parameters you have put on your yes? How will you grow your

no or maybe or half-yes into a full and confident yes to anything God may ask of you?

2. How are you nurturing your love for the Lord above all other loves (consider people, plans, status, accomplishments)?

3. What struggles do you foresee in your pursuit to remain pure and holy (physically, mentally, and emotionally) before the Lord? What will an accountability plan look like for you?

CHAPTER 8

Missions and Motherhood

Amy Bowman

From the General Editor

RAISING KIDS IS one of the most incredible, joy-filled gifts that God gives to mothers and fathers. Raising kids is also one of the hardest things that anyone will ever do. I know that before I became a mom, I never would have imagined that so much of me would be tied up in loving these little humans. I did not understand how, somehow, after you give birth or adopt, these small people graft themselves so immediately and deeply into who you are that you forget who you were before them.

This life-altering experience of sharing your heart with your kids holds true for most parents, whether missionaries or not. Yet, to be honest, on the mission field there are some unique challenges for parents as they seek to integrate their kids into their calling. On one hand, it is so easy to idolize the life we think our little humans deserve. On the field, far from home, we can succumb to the weight of guilt we are tempted to feel when we view our kids' lives overseas as missing out on what their lives would be back home. But on the other hand, it is equally easy to throw our lives and hearts into the work we are doing and neglect the beautiful work of discipling our own flock God has put under our care.

For these reasons, I am so grateful for my friend Amy Bowman's wise reflections on integrating parenting and missions without sacrificing either. Amy's advice for balancing ministry and motherhood rings so true to what I have seen on the mission field. I desperately wish that I could have observed her loving and discipling her kids overseas as I was learning this balancing act for myself. However, even though I did not get to see it on the mission field, I now get the fruit of watching her kids pouring into my own as the Lord has kindly planted our families together in the same place during this season of life and ministry. And I am so glad that you, reader, have the chance to hear and heed Amy's wise words as you prepare to go.

MISSIONS AND MOTHERHOOD

"Take them out." No one understood his words except me. I was crouched on a short stool with my four-year-old on one side and my two-year-old on the other, while my four-month-old tried to sleep in the sling where she was tied to my back. I felt like a human jungle gym instead of a mom sitting in church listening to my husband preach. The baby was getting fussy, and my toddler was whispering too loudly. So, in the middle of preaching in the local African dialect, he paused long enough to ask me in English to go ahead and take the kids outside. We got up and walked out, followed by a chicken and a small parade of a few other curious toddlers.

It may sound harsh, but it was not a mean-spirited request. My husband, Joshua, could sense that the kids were a little too much of a distraction for the rest of the villagers at church that morning, so he discretely encouraged me to "take them out" for the sake of the congregation. As I sat outside while my children played in the dirt and chased the chicken that had followed us out of the hut that served as the village church building, the thought crossed my mind: "Why did I even come today? It would have been easier just to sing some songs and read a Bible story to my children at home, while Joshua went to the village for the church meeting." .

As I reflected on that question, I came to realize that, yes, it *would* be easier. But it would not be obedience. When God called Joshua and me to go and share the gospel cross-culturally where the name of Christ was unknown, our children were not an after-thought. I knew God had called me to proclaim His goodness and salvation to this remote village. But I also knew that God called our whole family to this place and this task. I could not merely find ways to work and minister when it was convenient to leave the kids at home.

The Scriptures remind us in multiple places that the Creator of the universe is sovereign over the placement of our lives, "having determined allotted periods and the boundaries of [our] dwelling place" (Acts 17:26 ESV). For our family—including both Joshua and me along with our kids—during this season of life, the Lord had brought us to live in a village in Africa.

God knew that for my four children, living in Zambia would involve learning new things, experiencing new foods and culture, and even participating in our family's ministry as they grew in age and maturity. My job as their mother was to allow these kids to see the work God is doing and let them be a part of it at each stage of their lives.

For us, God had used the example of families He called to various places and tasks throughout the Scriptures to help us develop strong convictions about raising a family, even before arriving on the mission field. Let me share three of the passages that proved to be anchors for my heart as I sought to mother a family on mission.

A BIBLICAL BASIS FOR A FAMILY ON MISSION

The Bible is full of perspective-challenging stories, examples, and commands for both individuals and families who are called to follow Him. Even before we get to the global mission that is unleashed in the New Testament post-Pentecost, the Old Testament has much to say about how families are to function as conduits of God's purposes in His world.

The first formative passage that I want to look at is one that I had memorized at an early age, the Shema of Deuteronomy 6:4–9. It says:

> "Listen, Israel: The LORD our God, the LORD is one. Love the LORD your God with all your heart, with all your soul, and with all your strength. These words that I am giving you today are to be in your heart. Repeat them to your children. Talk about them when you sit in your house and when you walk along the road, when you lie down and when you get up. Bind them as a sign on your hand and let them be a symbol

on your forehead. Write them on the doorposts
of your house and on your city gates."

These verses reiterate the importance of teaching our children all throughout the day how to love the Lord. The requirement is that I am with my children. They need to watch me love God with all of my heart, soul, mind, and strength. They need to hear the truths of God over and over.

Seeing the faith and priorities of one's parents isn't a one-time lesson. I knew that these verses—along with many others like them—required me to be ready to teach my children the things of God and to show them how to love Him fully and bring Him glory. I wanted to teach them by the way they saw their father and me living that God has called us to be His ambassadors—especially among those who have never heard about Him.

My goal was not just for my children to respond to Jesus as their personal Savior. I wanted my children to see how God can use their lives in order to bring *many* to know Jesus as Savior. In order for that to happen, my children had to be present. They needed to see their parents loving and serving God first. And second, they needed to witness us faithfully loving others. This meant that, oftentimes, their naps were missed, their hands got dirty, their tongues tasted strange foods, and all the while, their little hearts learned to love those who didn't look like them. They got to learn the beauty of meeting and worshiping alongside of their brothers and sisters in Christ who lived in places that most of their American friends would likely never get to visit.

As much as I wish I could boast of consistently keeping this perspective of how blessed my kids were by all of these things, I have to admit that I often had to fight for it. In fact, I remember one day distinctly where I was pining for an easier lot for my kids and for me as their mom. It had been an especially exhausting season, and I was allowing myself to build a list of all the things that would be easier if I were raising my kids back in the U.S.

This brings us to the second passage that has shaped my view of parenting on mission. I was in full-on "get-me-out-of-here" mode the day that the Holy Spirit used Hebrews 11:15–16, a passage from my quiet time that morning, to convict me as the message jumped off the page and into my heart: "If they had been thinking of that land from which they had gone out, they would have had opportunity to return. But as it is, they desire a better country, that is, a heavenly one. Therefore God is not ashamed to be called their God, for he has prepared for them a city" (ESV).

Living cross-culturally without the ease of Western conveniences is often hard, challenging, and discouraging. If I had wanted to find an excuse to return to America, I could have given you a list an arm's length long and felt completely justified in buying six return tickets to America. But the Lord used these verses from Hebrews to remind me of what had brought us to Zambia in the first place: I wanted something different. I wanted my children to experience and know the God in whom they believed as they saw Him at work in the lives of the people He called us to live among.

While there are many more passages that I would love to reflect on, I want to share one final verse that proved formative for my vision of parenting on the mission field. In Psalm 37:3, it is written: "Trust in the LORD and do what is good; dwell in the land and live securely." I simply needed to do four things: trust, do good, dwell, and live confidently. If I wanted my children to experience God at work in their midst, it would have to start with their mother fully trusting in the Lord. I had to trust that this village, this community of new believers, the life He called us to live, was God's best plan for my children.

Trusting God and daily walking with Him in prayer and Bible reading enabled me to dwell as the psalmist describes above. But how does one really dwell like this? How do trust, prayer, and Bible reading lead a person to true dwelling and not just become ritualized, spiritual habit formation? As the psalmist uses them above, it seems that it means to trust and enjoy the place that you have been planted, not just because of the place itself, but because of the One who is with you. For my time overseas, *dwelling* meant being fully present with God and where He had put me. It meant not constantly looking back with longing to be in a different place or surrounded by different people. I had to put down roots and fully embrace the place where God called my family to live. As I trusted the One who called me, lived obediently, and enjoyed His plan, then I was able to live securely and confidently—not because I had everything under control, but because I knew the One who does. It allowed my children to dwell in the only place they knew to call home.

Building off of these basic biblical foundations, I have come to think of parenting cross-culturally differently than I used to. I am grateful for the chance to write some of these lessons down because it has forced me again—even though we are in a new season of life and ministry—to reconsider the framework for parenting that the Lord has been working into me during many previous seasons. It is a joy to offer you a few of those often hard-wrought lessons that have come to shape my view of parenting on mission before you go.

PRACTICAL ADVICE

Now as we enter this section, I want you to hear me clearly: I do not claim to have perfect children. Phenomenal children? Yes! But perfect? No. Likewise, I did not do everything right in the way I taught and raised my children overseas. Unfortunately, I didn't even always follow the advice I am giving you in this chapter! We learned some lessons the hard way. We went through seasons of intense difficulty in our parenting and in our ministry. So as we move into this next section where I am laying out some principles for raising kids cross-culturally, I would ask you to hear me offering this advice humbly—born of both my successes in parenting and my failures—to you as you discern how to raise your kids. I am praying that the Spirit would use these words that I wish someone had shared with me before I left for the field.

Let your children be present and involved in ministry.

Find ways—both noteworthy and minuscule—for your children to have a role in your ministry. In the bush of Africa, our toddlers knew when we went to a village to teach the Bible, their job was to open the windows of our Land Cruiser and greet everyone in the local language as we entered. While this may seem small, we shared with them that there were few cars that passed through these rural villages. Their smiling faces, then, would alert people to the fact that those who were in the car were there for ministry and that the Bible study would begin soon.

Likewise, when we went to church, I would tell each child that they had the job of smiling, shaking hands, and eating the yummy lunch after the service that had been graciously prepared for our family. These small roles involved the kids by calling them to use their smiling faces to create a hospitable welcome for those we had come to love. They and their smiles and greetings were part of the work.

As they got older, and when we were living in South Asia, my school-age daughters would accompany me to the inner-city slum as I taught evangelistic health lessons to women. They knew their job was to entertain the babies and toddlers close by so the moms could hear the gospel and not be distracted by their children. Each of our children traveled at different times with Joshua, either on a camping trip in Africa to an unreached village or by train in Asia to a city to encourage local believers.

When your children see the integral role they personally have in your family's calling, it will encourage their hearts when they miss family and friends back in the States. If your teenager is closely connected to the work and people with whom you are ministering, it solidifies the need and call of God on your family to stay when it is lonely. Helping them to see the eternal value of their work will also help them to endure when they are tempted to focus on how they may be missing out on things their American peers get to enjoy.

Different seasons in your family—and different personalities in your children—will affect the amount of time the entire family can be involved. Involving toddlers in ministry is going to look different than involving teenagers. A healthy balance is essential, but let your family be characterized by everyone being a part of ministry overseas. Don't let fear, lack of planning, or an idea that "this is the way it has always been done" keep you from involving your children in seeing God at work. For one of our Stateside assignments, I remember my children being offended because a well-meaning church member asked my two school-age children how they felt about their parents being missionaries. My son replied, "I'm a missionary too. I go with my dad to the village all the time to tell them about Jesus."

Resist the mindset that you are depriving your children by raising them overseas.

In the beginning, when you are caught up in the excitement and adventure of life abroad, you might not find yourself regularly thinking about what you are missing out on back home. But at some point, the temptation to see your children's lives as riddled with sacrifices will likely rear its head. It might not plague you until your school-age or teenage children are packing to return to your home overseas after time in the States. They may have to watch their cousins join soccer teams and join all the clubs at school, knowing that most likely their lives back on the field will look very different.

Discouragement and concern that you are depriving your children of something by living far from home can slowly creep in your mind and begin to discourage your heart. Picking up your cross at times will look like laying down the comfortable conveniences of the Western world, but even harder, it at times looks like asking your kids to do so as well.

There are many good things that might be sacrificed on the altar of obedience to which the Lord is calling you. Your obedience might require missing the extended family vacation each summer or birthday parties with cousins or getting to participate in school musicals.

Now, don't get me wrong. There are very real emotional and familial costs to this obedience, and we must not pretend that they don't exist. But when those reminders of what your family is missing out on threaten to overwhelm you, do the hard work of also listing the blessings and joys that you would be missing out on if you were not where the Lord has called you. First among those things is the joy of serving King Jesus. But every context also comes with its own unique blend of joys and opportunities that are real blessings in themselves. Think about the privilege of your kids getting to see brothers and sisters from a different place and culture worshiping the same God as they do back home. Think about the advantages that come from growing up in a multilingual environment. Think about the fact that they see the value of the gospel trumping any cost it might require to cling to it.

Constantly remind yourself and your children that, although it is costly, it is worth it. My children may not have a trophy from childhood sports participation, but they will have a wealth of experiences that will impact their worldview for the rest of their lives. They will realize the value of a person is determined by their image-bearing soul and not on the basis of the brand of jeans they wear. Missionary kids also often connect on a deeper level with those around them, having developed the habit of seeing needs an average person may overlook. They will have relationships with people who treat them like family not because of blood relations but because of the unity forged by the gospel. Of course, there is a difference between a childhood on the mission field and one in America, but make sure to see, count, and be grateful for the blessings that God has knit into this upbringing for your children.

Intentionally enable and encourage your children to make national friends.

While it may take a little bit of extra time to investigate ways that are culturally appropriate for kids to spend time with their peers, it is absolutely worth the effort. Find the activities that children their age are involved in and get them plugged in. As they begin to integrate with other kids and see life through their eyes, they will develop more comfort in the culture and make friends of their own.

Now, it probably needs to be pointed out that cultures differ in what is acceptable play among young children. Things that are tolerable in your host culture may be abhorrent to your family's convictions. For instance, in Africa, boys often fight for fun, and children are left unsupervised for long periods of time. Since I didn't want my two-year-old to learn that playing with friends meant hitting them with sticks, I had to seek out families with kids who were less aggressive. This also usually involved opportunities for me to find a mom with whom I could sit and talk while keeping an eye on our young boys as they played together.

In another season and location, during language school in South Asia, Joshua and I needed concentrated opportunities in the community to practice what we were learning in class. Instead of leaving the kids at home, we enrolled three of our children in tennis lessons so they could meet friends their age and we could practice talking with the parents during their lesson time. Ministry opportunities and socialization of your children can go hand in hand in these ways and countless others.

Eventually your kids will begin to pick up on these patterns of socialization and ministry opportunity as well. When we moved to a new city, my daughter noticed the girls who were kind to her on the playground in our apartment complex also took roller-skating lessons on Saturday mornings. Not only did this allow her to be around national girls building friendships with them, but it also opened opportunities for me to establish friendships with three other moms, eventually enabling me to share the gospel with each of them in their homes. Likewise, after we had to move apartment complexes, everyone knew Luke because he played soccer and cricket every evening with the neighbors, which led to my meeting more women.

Some seasons required us to change our traditional family routine to allow our family life to intersect with nationals. We started having afternoon tea times and later dinner so our kids could play in the park with our neighbors in the evenings. In both places our family raised our children, being involved in our local community allowed nationals to see a picture of the difference the gospel makes in our home. They saw us live out the gospel's implications as they saw me lovingly correct my children, praise them, or help them control their anger on the tennis court when losing a match.

A commonality among all mothers in every culture is their children. Hindu, Sikh, and Muslim women would ask me why my kids obeyed or how I could be patient when they did not. My response was almost always, "Well, because the Christian Scripture teaches me to parent my children differently. Can I tell you about it?" Such an invitation resulted in being welcomed into the home of a Sikh family because she was curious about why our family interactions were so different. I ended up sharing the gospel with her and giving her a New Testament—all because she noticed something different in the way that I related to my children and they related to me. Let your children be a gateway into your communities. They are bridges, not hindrances, to sharing the gospel with those you came to serve.

Do not neglect discipling your children in your home.

When you are one of the few lights in a dark place, you must constantly find ways to input biblical truth and sound doctrine into your family. Most evenings we read and prayed together as a family. Sometimes we sang, prayed, and cried. During our Bible time each morning in homeschool, we memorized Scripture. As I look back on the variety of family worship times throughout our kids' childhood, they are the sweetest memories.

However, we never wanted our kids to think family worship was synonymous with worshiping with the local body of believers. It is a complement, but not a substitution. The church is the reason we go, so just because it is hard, uncomfortable, and long does not justify me staying home with my children. Even in a different language that my children may not fully understand, there is value in them worshiping with the body of Christ. Many Sundays, I had to whisper in my children's ears what the next words of a song were or what the individual sharing a testimony was saying. They had words or phrases to listen for during the sermon.

When they were teenagers, we attended a local fellowship that had an English-speaking youth group where they were able to discuss Scripture with peers. It is challenging because you often feel you must be everything for your children. Some Sundays, I would have loved to drop everyone off in kids' ministry or have a youth leader available to pour into my struggling young person. Keep fighting. You are not enough, but your God who called you is. He will provide exactly what your children need at the exact time.

An aspect of discipleship is transparency. As vulnerable as it seems, let your children hear you cry out to God to provide for your needs as well as theirs—physical and emotional needs that come from living in a host culture. I cannot recount how many times I prayed for God to send a friend to my lonely teen or an opportunity for them that I couldn't orchestrate. But God did. Let your children see you needy, but also let them see Who meets your needs. It helps them learn to trust their heavenly Father.

Let your children hear testimonies of national brothers and sisters—including their suffering.

Allowing your children to know nationals well encourages them when they are called to do hard things. Our instincts as parents might be to protect and shelter our children from harm and suffering. It is our biblical responsibility to care well for our children. However, letting them hear about the cost of discipleship in the lives of those you are ministering among allows them to have a front-row seat to see the character of God. Hearing how God provided in miraculous ways for our national partners was a powerful testimony in our children's lives. The persecuted believer was not just a person in a book; it was the father of my child's friend.

When our family experienced illness or loneliness, my children drew strength from the fact that they had seen the faithfulness of God in the lives of those around them. They knew the same God who helped Uncle Kumar escape his persecutors is the same God who is with them when their brother had emergency surgery. My children witnessed the power of the gospel to transform lives and families as they loved and shared life with those who once were far from Christ. My daughters helped Aunty Renu teach children about Jesus in the slum because it had been twelve years since she had seen her own son. When Renu became a follower of Christ, her Muslim husband moved to another city with her only son and she never saw him again. My girls wept.

My oldest son took an Uber weekly to meet a national pastor who waited for him outside his village. Caleb would hop on the back of his motorcycle and ride into the village to help him with English classes as an outreach. Stories from Uncle Sunil, a former idol maker, were etched on his heart. Following Jesus was costly, yet worth it. Luke had Uncle Sumit wrapped around his finger when we first moved to South Asia. As he grew older he learned how Sumit's life was changed radically after believing the gospel, so he knows it can change anyone. Knowing the power of the gospel to save has been imprinted on my children's hearts, so they pray even now for lost friends to be saved because they have seen it happen before. No family is too wrecked by sin that the gospel cannot save.

BEING A FAMILY ON MISSION IS WORTH IT

I want to close by telling you the end of the story that we began with. That day that I was sitting outside of the village church in the dirt with the chickens I was tempted to wonder: "Was it even worth it for me to come today?" But when Joshua finished preaching and the Zambians had filed out, the kids and I joined the traditional circle outside of the church, shaking hands and singing.

I spoke to the women as my children ran and played with the other kids. We ate a traditional meal that was graciously prepared for us. Then we loaded our family back into the truck to return to our home. Caleb and Abbie smiled and waved out of the windows. Anna was content in her infant seat. The kids drifted off to sleep despite the bumpy dirt road, and I smiled. As we left that village in the rearview mirror until the next visit, I was already fully convinced that it was worth the trip on all counts. I wouldn't want to miss this. Not for the sake of ease, not for the sake of comfort, not for the sake of anything.

God lovingly calls us. It is for our good. Somehow in His grace, He allowed my family with all our imperfections to bring Him glory by calling us to plant our lives cross-culturally for a season. I want to be clear with you: Life on the field will be hard, mamas. There will be illness, exhaustion, and heat. You will ask yourself, "Why?" But please hear me cheering for you. You must keep your focus on the end goal. Your children are watching you love God with all your heart, soul, and strength. These little humans will have a front-row seat to see God's glory and the power of the gospel. Your children may not fully understand your reasoning, but there is no better way for them to see you genuinely believe He is worthy than for them to be right alongside you.

DISCUSS AND REFLECT

1. What are your fears or concerns regarding raising a family cross-culturally?

2. What Scriptures might you meditate on to aide you in submitting those fears to the will of God for your life?

3. Are there any women in your life presently you can glean wisdom from regarding parenting cross-culturally? If so, think of several practical questions you can ask them applicable to your family.

4. Evaluate your heart's attitude regarding children and ministry. How have you viewed children and family life in regard to your life calling?

CHAPTER 9

Fear and Anxiety

Nina Buser

From the General Editor

I HAVE KNOWN about the missionary training work that Nina and her husband, Brooks, have been providing through Radius International for quite some time. However, in the last few years, my husband and I have been able to see with our own eyes the fruitful work the Busers, along with their team at Radius, are doing from up close. It is even more impressive in person than the accounts of their work we had heard. The team members at Radius are using their gifts, training, and experience with which they have been entrusted to equip those going to some of the hardest, most gospel-deprived places on the face of the earth.

I have an immense amount of respect for Brooks and Nina. What they have put their hands to the plow to do is much-needed work. However, one of the greatest things about people doing important work is when you meet them and find them to be gospel-humbled people who desire to listen well, invest in those around them, and seek to serve instead of being served. I believe Nina to be that type of person.

Relatively speaking, I have not spent much time with Nina. However, even in the short time we have had, I found myself wanting to pour out my stories to her, listen to her stories, and glean from her wisdom—especially as it relates to dealing with facing the task of church planting among unreached people groups with trust and courage. Fear and anxiety are inevitable parts of walking into the unknowns of missionary life. However, I pray that you will be encouraged as you read Nina's wisdom and advice about laying our fear and our anxiety at the Father's feet.

FEAR AND ANXIETY

In January 2001, my husband and I, along with our seven-month-old son, loaded up our minivan with our possessions stuffed in and around us and left sunny San Diego for snowy Oregon. I'll never forget the white-knuckle driving through the Truckee overpass with snow piled high and having to help put on snow chains around the tires of our van for the first time in my life. Why the crazy move? My husband, Brooks, and I had made the decision together with the confirmation of our church that we would obey Matthew 28 and the authority of Christ to "go . . . and make disciples of all nations" (v. 19a). We knew without a doubt we would need serious training in order to be equipped to do this task, so we set off for the first phase of missionary training. This training would teach us how to learn language and culture. It would teach us to navigate the complexities of communication when no written language had yet been developed. It would help us to learn how to teach literacy, build a house and possibly an airstrip, do medical work, and cook from scratch, among other things.

With all that we were about to do and learn, what were the thoughts that took up most of my mind? Oddly enough, I vividly remember one particular concern that kept rolling around in my head and heart: "Oh my word, I have not been away from our son since he was born and now for this training, I will be putting him in day care four hours a day?" The anxious thoughts did not stop there, but would often snowball on to thoughts like: "What if someday he leaves us for boarding school?"

Looking back now, it is almost humorous: here we were, in the midst of this monumental task of preparing for every conceivable circumstance we would encounter on the field where danger and uncertainty would face us daily, and yet it was the need to entrust my infant son to four hours of day care that had me anxious and concerned. How did my thoughts move so quickly from day care to the potential that we might one day need to send him to board-ing school? *Fear.*

In the middle of all kinds of unknowns that stood before us, my heart was myopically focused in on a single aspect of my life: my son. My heart would literally ache at the thought of having to say goodbye to him because he was one of the most precious things in my world. I would gaze lovingly at our beautiful baby boy who was all smiles and giggles and contentment—and right in that very moment, the weight of the future when he might have to leave us in the jungle and go off to school would crash upon me and steal my joy. It wasn't that I didn't want to serve the Lord. I was completely willing to go. My fear wasn't over my own well-being, but his. What if I couldn't protect him?

Now, as the time in training got underway, I did come to recognize that day care was a blessing. It allowed me the freedom to sit undistracted in the classes that would help me greatly in the future. The training did a lot to excite me about all the things the Lord was going to allow us to be a part of. I got more and more excited to join Him in the work that He was doing to make sure that people from another language group would one day be standing before the throne praising God.

Still, all too often, my fears would come rushing back as I thought about what this life might mean for my son. I was all for laying down my life for Jesus, but the thought of any sort of hardship involving my son had my stomach in knots. I would pray to God, "Lord, I will give you my life gladly for the sake of the gospel, but please don't ask me to give up my son." Mentally, I was drawing a line in the sand that I was afraid God would cross. I was channeling all of my fear and anxiety of the unknown onto this particular fear of having to give up or lose this boy who was in my arms.

I talk with women all the time who want so badly to serve the Lord in church planting and yet they find themselves struggling with cycles of fear. For mothers, many times this fear centers around their children. For some women, there is a deep, very real fear of loneliness, of missing family and friends, of getting sick, or of struggling with health concerns. For many single women I speak to, there is a persistent struggle of fearing the prospect of never getting married because of their choices to go on the field.

All of us have our specific lines in the sand we don't want the Father to ask us to cross.

During the specific times when I would seesaw from excitement about the future to dread of the unknown, I would get to the end of my rapidly fraying rope and force my mind to stop replaying the "what-if" loops. Instead of merely trying in my own strength to quiet or redirect my thoughts, I found that it was better to actively refill and refocus my mind by seeking comfort in the Word.

One of the verses that has brought me great comfort is Colossians 1:17: "He is before all things, and by him all things hold together." It is so simple and yet so profound. I have poured over this verse so many times it is now etched in my heart, and it reflexively comes out of me as a reaction to fear. There is so much solid truth in this one verse that reminds me of His character and who I am in Him. As it has ministered so faithfully to me, I want in these brief pages to unpack some of what I have learned from this verse for you. I share this in hopes that it will likewise offer solace to you as you face the various heart-responses involved in preparing to go.

REST IN WHO HE IS

The first phrase of this verse is arresting. Its beautiful simplicity speaks of God's inconceivable eternality: "He is before all things." He—the One who is and will forever be—always has been Himself, even before anything else existed.

And while Paul here merely refers to God as "he," we know from the rest of the Bible that this "he" is the God who has revealed Himself to His creation throughout time. Throughout the pages of Scripture—and in the dust and dirt of history—God has shown His people that He is unchanging in His goodness. He is also the omniscient, omnipresent, omnipotent One who has always been and is.

When I took time to realize that this "he" who is before creation is and always has been all of those "omnis," it began to provide incredible peace for me in times of anxiousness. This verse is obviously saying that God has existed before anything else. But if this God is unchanging—which the rest of Scripture attests to—then that means that He is not only the God who knows all things now, but He is also the God who knew all things before He brought the universe into being. The Creator of the universe who existed before anything was created knew, knows, and will know everything—past, present, and future all together.

This means that there is nothing that has ever or will ever surprise God. What assurance His eternality provides as I realize that it means there is nothing in my life that will catch Him off guard! He cannot be tricked or fooled. He will never be shocked by a circumstance that comes up. He knows everything before it will happen, good and bad. He preexisted any situation that might befall me, and He is sovereign over my circumstances. This reality of God's eternality and omniscience has proven so grounding for me when fear about the future rears its ugly head. It reminds me to heed Paul's observation in Romans 8:32: "He did not even spare his own Son but gave him up for us all. How will he not also with him grant us everything?"

This plays out in very real ways and in the face of very real fears. I mentioned earlier that some of my greatest fears as we prepared for the mission field revolved around my son. Now, just like any mother, I know that there is not a soul on this planet who will ever love our son the way Brooks and I do. Yet the love we have for our son is but a fraction of how much our Father loves him. This One who loves my son even more than I do is the same One who knows the future and has already given us the strength in Christ to face it.

But God's eternal omniscience is not the only comfort that comes from Colossians 1:17. This verse also reinforces our confidence in His omnipotence and omnipresence as it says, "and by him all things hold together." The eternal, all-knowing God of the universe is everywhere and holding all things together. There is no corner of the world that I can go where He cannot fully see me. There is no hut in the middle of the jungle, or tent in the desert, or room in a faraway country where I can be hidden from Him. And not only can I not hide from Him physically, but even my inmost thoughts are clear to Him as He knows me better than I know myself: "Before a word is on my tongue, you know all about it, LORD" (Ps. 139:4). I can rest in the fact that God knows my fears even before I voice them.

There is deep rest to be found in this God who is omniscient and omnipresent. And on top of that, He is also omnipotent. Not only does He know everything and see everything, but our heavenly Father is also powerful over all things. He not only created the universe and all that is within it, but He is literally holding it all together—every corner of it. He is holding the heavens in place and also holding my life in His hands. And not only my life, but also the lives of my husband and my son.

This reality provided solace to me when fears of the future and unknowns would crowd in around me. It provided comfort when I clung to the truth that God held my son in His loving hands when I could not. It proved enough whether I was worried about what I would miss while he was in the nursery or whether I was anxious about whether I would be able to get medical attention if he hurt himself or got sick in the jungle. The same God provided the same peace no matter the circumstances.

Sister, let me encourage you to cling to the simple-yet-profound truth that the things that are most precious to us on this earth are held by Him. This means all of our fears of the future are not only known by Him, but His plans for the future are already set. This God who has already given me all things in Christ will provide me with the peace that comes from His presence, which will allow me to rest in Him.

Throughout our training and our time on the field, one thought often kept me going: if the omniscient, omnipresent, and omnipotent God has called us to go, I can trust Him with all that obedience entails. The place my anxiety goes to die is at the feet of this God who is before all things and by whom all things hold together.

Now, I admit that the journey to learning to lay down my fears and anxiousness is much easier to write about than it is to actually fight. I am daily continuing to learn to surrender to God, and my life is still marked—as it is for all of us—by fits and starts of successfully remembering to find my peace in God and His unchanging goodness. If you are struggling with these same fears as you prepare to go, I can sympathize!

But I also pray that the Lord would minister to you through the simple, profound beauty of Colossians 1:17. From the place of confidence that the Lord has given me through this passage, I have come to five practices that have helped me practically put down my fears and pick up biblical truths. I pray that the following advice will serve you in that same way.

FEARS ABOUND, BUT I AM CALLED TO GO

In my role at Radius, I often have women coming to me for advice about whether or not they should go into missions. Most have certain fears that they are trying to reconcile as they weigh out if this is what the Lord has for them. Typically—born out of my own battles against fear—I will give them the five pieces of advice for laying down our fears that I want to close this chapter with: consider the cost; get good training; memorize Scripture; keep a prayer journal; and read missionary biographies.

Go with Knowledge

Many women on the mission field point back to hearing a powerful sermon, a testimony, or being convicted by Scripture as their motivation toward missions. I myself was a new believer attending a missions conference when I remember hearing about unreached people groups. I remember thinking, "Of course they are dying and going to hell; no one has told them the gospel!" While I remember being willing to go even as a new believer, it was years before the Lord sent me. For some people it takes giving God their willingness to go, while for others they express always having experienced an emotional pull toward missions.

Whatever the case, I truly believe it is important to really understand, as best as possible, the cost of what it takes to plant a church among an unreached people group. This may seem counterintuitive to purposely think about things that could be potentially dangerous and bring up fears when we are talking about how to deal with fear and anxiety. However, the decision to lay one's life down to take the gospel to the ends of the earth needs to be approached with sober judgment. There is a reason that the last places on earth are unreached. These places are hard to get to and hard to live in. I truly believe that it is not for everyone. There are certain things that you must die to. Sometimes the things are dreams of marriage, family, good health, or comfortable living. Again, this might seem contrary to dealing with fears and anxieties as I'm asking you to consider the dangers and isolation that you may face. It is only in acknowledging the reality of the hardships to come that we can surrender our fears truly to the Lord and trust in His plan, understanding that hardships most likely will be a part of them.

For those who sign up to go and think of it as an adventure, I would caution them that the "adventure" quickly wears off. There are sickness, isolation, loss of family, loneliness, and being misunderstood or mistreated that will all be in store for you. If you haven't faced these as a reality to which you are entering into yet, you need to. You must come face-to-face with your fears and worries to surrender all of your future, your rights, and your dreams to the Lord. This is a process that will need to be repeated many times as new fears come up or old fears are dredged up.

Go with Preparation

Part of counting the cost before you go may involve your pursuit of good training. Unfortunately, there are many people who come home from the field earlier than they intended because they weren't prepared. Having a passion for the Lord and a plane ticket does not sufficiently prepare one to deal with the varying trials that come up on the mission field. When someone has gone through training to handle difficult situations, it gives them a way to handle what is to come, especially if the training is difficult in and of itself. I could not imagine doing what the Lord called us to do without first having gone through the training we had.

Some of the training dealt with practical, daily, and even mundane types of things. But looking back, now I see how God prepared me even through those little things that I thought nothing of at the time. One small example is when we were in the missionary training school, I remember having to haul water down the hallway to wash our dishes every night. It was years later, when we made it to the tribe we served among, that I found myself again hauling water over a distance to wash dishes. God in His providence knew that even though it was harder in my new living situation, I at least felt a little bit prepared because I had hauled water before. I could certainly do it again.

Training should be a tool that helps you truly count the cost before you go. As you sit in classes it should bring up things that maybe you haven't even considered yet. I can't tell you how many women tell me, "I didn't know what I didn't know," after listening to classes on suffering, culture and language acquisition, marriage, and parenting. So many of the missionaries who come home discouraged often do so because they were caught off guard by the difficulties they encountered on the field. They didn't know how hard it would be and, not surprisingly, were unable to handle their fears and anxieties when they were in the middle of dealing with them.

Of course, good missions training does not mean that you will be able to avoid all trials. Our wise and responsible preparation does not mean that we will avoid any kind of undesirable circumstances on the field. We cannot simply prepare ourselves away from every situation we might fear; but we can, in wisdom, prepare ourselves as best we can and recognize our need to trust God with the rest. I am clearly biased, but I believe a program like Radius International is a wonderful way for missionary candidates to work through as much of this preparation for the field as possible while also cultivating hearts that trust the Lord in the hard things that they will yet face.

Go with God's Truth

Is it me, or do the worst fears come in the dark of night? Usually these would be fears that, during the day, we might be able to push aside with busyness and distractions. I remember vividly at times, before we went to the field, when I would lie in bed some nights chewing on a particular fear until I worked myself into a full frenzy. I somehow had a special talent for drawing up stories in my mind that could give Tolkien a run for his money. In order to get out of the crazy sagas playing in my mind, I learned the best way to reign in the madness was to focus on truth. I would meditate on Philippians 4:8: "Finally brothers and sisters, whatever is true, whatever is honorable, whatever is just, whatever is pure, whatever is lovely, whatever is commendable—if there is any moral excellence and if there is anything praiseworthy—dwell on these things." I love the word *dwell* here. There is so much wisdom in dwelling on the *actual* truth of God's promises instead of on what *might* come.

I have found that usually the fears that are the strongest for us are directly related to the things that are most precious to us. For me, it was our son and the health of our family. For others it can be singleness, leaving family, or even the comforts of their own culture. I was fortunate enough to have many godly teachers and mentors around me that continually pointed me back to Scripture. They constantly encouraged me to memorize it, meditate on it, sing it, and hide it in my heart.

As I practiced this, the Lord faithfully showed me where I was holding onto something so tightly that it had become an idol. I was amazed that good things like marriage, children, health, and success so quickly became idols in my heart. It was and is something I continually need to bring before the Lord. I remember listening to a sermon a while back where the pastor said that you can tell when something has become an idol when that thing gets touched by adversity and your fears stir in you the most. I'm not saying that every fear is related to idolatry, but it can definitely reveal things in our hearts that we need to surrender over to the Lord.

Go with Prayer

Almost as soon as I had become a believer, I began to practice prayer journaling. For some this might seem like a daunting task, but it really is quite simple. When I found myself in a pit of anxiety, I would write out my prayers in bullet points. Once I had written them out on paper, I would add in Scripture that addressed my concerns and focused my mind on them.

Despite the twinge of embarrassment that would sometimes come from recording my fears in black-and-white, I found myself often moved to praise God that He already knew my inmost thoughts—even before I wrote them out. And because of His omniscience, there is nothing that I could write that would shock God. The great thing that happens as we write our prayers is that we are able to admit to ourselves what we are feeling or think-ing, to get it all out before the Lord, and to see what we may be unconsciously carrying in our hearts throughout our days. Often during these prayer times I would find myself reading what I wrote and then thinking, "Wow, Lord, I didn't even know I was carrying that." Often it was a sin that I was holding on to and needed to confess or a worry that I would keep coming back to.

Once I was able to see the sin or worry on paper, I would go back to Scripture and find truth that would lead me to confess or take my thoughts captive. Sometimes in the deep distress I even prayed Scripture back to the Lord, as my words did not seem to be sufficient for all I was feeling. For example, I would pray the truths of Mark 10:29–30 and Matthew 6:34 back to God: "Lord, thank You that no one who has left home or brothers or sisters or mother or father or children for the gospel will fail to receive more in heaven. Help me to be faithful today with what You have given me and leave tomorrow's worries to tomorrow. Thank You that *You* know the cost of leaving the comforts of home and fam-ily behind for something that is going to echo into eternity. I am weak, Lord; give me Your strength to face today."

Go with Past Saints

Something else that I encourage women to do is to read missionary biographies. There is something greatly encouraging in the stories of how the Lord uses very ordinary but faithful men and women to take the gospel to where it hasn't been preached before. Not only does reading about the hardships they faced sober us, but seeing their love and faith in our heavenly Father in the midst of their trials emboldens us to trust God as well. Drawing on the faith of those who have gone before us, especially in the midst of dealing with our own fears, can bring great comfort and encouragement.

Sister, you are not alone in your fears. There is a great cloud of witnesses cheering us on for the sake of the glory of the King. I love the exhortation of Amy Carmichael's prayer: "Teach us, good Lord, to serve Thee as Thou deservest; . . . , to fight and not to heed the wounds, to toil and not to seek for rest; to labor and not to ask for any reward save that of knowing that we do Thy will, O Lord our God."[9] Oh, that we would not seek any reward other than doing His will.

GO WITH TRUST

I would love to tell you that I never struggled with fears, but I can't. I can, however, vouch for the fact that with each trial we faced God was right there with us in the midst of it. He provided what we needed when we got malaria. He was there during the seasons of isolation. He brought comfort as I said goodbye to some dreams and replaced them with new ones. He used the trials and persecution to strengthen new believers and grow the church in ways that still brings tears to my eyes. He met my fears straight on and taught me that I really can trust Him with things that are most precious to me.

When things don't make earthly sense, His plan really is good. Sometimes it was deliverance from the storms, other times it was provision in the storms, and often it was His peace through the storms. Most encouraging of all is there is so much more to come for those who are called His children. On paper, saying goodbye to loved ones and giving up comforts to live in a faraway land with hostile people is crazy. Only in the light of eternity is living a life of sacrifice for a Savior who sacrificed all worth it. It is when we hold so tightly to this world that we lose sight of the one to come. Having an eternal perspective is the only way to bring incomprehensible peace and hope in the midst of fears and anxiety. It really is worth it because He is worthy.

DISCUSS AND REFLECT

1. What are fears that come to mind when you think of going to the mission field?

2. When you think of these fears, have they revealed any areas where they might actually be idols? One way to tell if you have idols is that if _____ gets taken away, then your whole world will fall apart. Our hearts are "idol factories"; we all have things we need to keep surrendering to the Lord.

3. If you have read any missionary biographies, what are some examples of their faith that have inspired you? If you haven't read any, what are some books that you would like to read?

4. How do you typically work through fears in your life? What are some ways you can do better at dealing with them?

5. What verse or verses encourage you the most when you are facing fears? What is it about the verse or verses that helps you?

CHAPTER 10

The Spiritual Patterns of a Missionary

Emily Bennett

From the General Editor

DEAR READER, IF you have found your way to this final chapter, I am assuming that you have probably already worked through some of the sage advice that the ladies of the previous chapters have recorded for you. I hope that you have been both encouraged and challenged by their stories and their commitment to making the name of Jesus known, following Him no matter what the apparent costs involve.

It has been the heartbeat of this whole book to provide soon-to-be missionaries with the wise advice of ladies who are a few steps down the road from where you are right now. Hopefully, you have already benefitted from how they have addressed and highlighted some of the unique ways missionary lives are affected by the types of cross-cultural environments you will soon inhabit.

However, as we close this project, we want to be sure that we do not inadvertently give the impression that the uniqueness of the missionary life indicates that it is built on a different foundation than Christians called to minister back home. Lest you come away thinking that the missionary life is somehow fundamentally different than the lives of brothers and sisters who are following Jesus in what He has called them to back home, this final chapter intends to remind us of the calling we share with disciples everywhere: to walk closely with Jesus and to follow Him in all that we do, wherever we are.

You may already be hearing echoes of the chapter on singleness, where Sydney reminded us that no matter the location or situation, the instructions that Jesus gave His disciples in Matthew 22:37 remain the first and greatest commandment: to *love* the Lord your God with all your heart, soul, and mind. We do this by *abiding* in Him and *remembering* the good work He has done on our behalf.

Reader, I don't know where you are right now. You may be currently debating whether God is calling you to missionary life. You may be training somewhere in preparation for what He is calling you to. Or maybe you've just arrived on the mission field and are reading this chapter while sitting on your version of that stained yellow couch that I spoke of in the introduction, wondering what you just got yourself into.

But no matter where you are—no matter what concerns, tasks, or questions you find yourself engaged with—priority number one in your life should be to love God and faithfully abide in Him. This central calling cannot be trumped or usurped by any other issue you may face on the field. In this final chapter, then, I want to share with you some of my own stories, struggles, and advice as it comes to loving God and abiding in Him, and how it is essential for missionary life.

LOVING THE LORD DRIVES SERVING THE LORD

If you and I had the chance to get to know one another, you would quickly realize that I am naturally a doer. On the field I loved filling up my time with language and meeting with women, and enjoyed the rhythms of teaching English throughout the week. I loved getting up early in the morning, running hard all day, and then crashing into my pillow at night, exhausted from all the activity and tasks of the last twenty-four hours.

In 2016, however, I found myself in a new season of life. I had just given birth and now I had three children under the age of four in my home. My husband and I felt the constant tension of needing to care for, love, and invest in our kids while also needing to do the ministry tasks the Lord put before us in our community. The Lord had blessed us with the chance to run and develop a school, which resulted in us being connected to more people than we had time to meet with already. Adding responsibilities of the home and family to the business pressures and ministry, we were quickly and often overwhelmed at the task that extended beyond our capacities. Yet in the gracious sovereignty of God, He used this season of life to remind us that He made us to be finite humans with limited hours per day to work with. Our limitations were not to be understood as a sign of our failure, but a reminder of our dependence.

Now, I hate admitting this, but I am going to be honest with you here. Even though I know that all my efforts are dependent upon Christ to bring in a harvest, I often struggle to accept that if I do more work, it may not necessarily result in more fruit. I so quickly slip back into patterns of working harder, which all too

often means abiding less. But when I do, I find the Lord reminding me of the precious gift He gave me in 2016 as He allowed me
to see how much He can do when I choose to abide.

In that season, our life stage and circumstances caused me to
spend a lot more time in my home than usual. With three young
children and a year wrought with sickness and instability throughout the country, I had much more time when all I could do in
ministry was to pray. I found myself sitting on my balcony while
my newborn slept in the other room, looking out on our city of
six million people, and asking the Lord to give me His eyes to see
the people around me as Jesus did—like sheep without a shepherd.
That year I prayed for my Middle Eastern friends more than I ever
had before.

The beautiful thing that the Lord did during those times of
prayer was to remind me that the very miracle I was pleading with
Him to do in my friends' lives was the miracle He had accom-
plished in bringing my own sin-dead heart to life. The more I
pressed into prayer, the more deeply I began to appreciate my own
salvation. The more I appreciated my own salvation and asked
the Lord to bring my friends to eternal life, the more burdened
I became to share the hope of the gospel with them. My own
expanding gratitude for the gospel resulted in an ever-deepening
burden to invite my friends to share in this gospel.

In those hours of rocking sleeping babies, I did what I could. I
brought before the Father the names of the women I had met with
and begged God to have mercy on them. I asked God to show me
the specific women around me He was working in. I asked Him
to bring them to my door and to multiply the fruitfulness of the
hours I had with them. I asked that He would go ahead of me and

allow me to use the time that He gave me with them to bear fruit in both of our lives.

God was indeed faithful to do these things. I was in this season of coming to terms with how much I am dependent upon Him to maximize the impact of my limited time—and that is precisely the season He used to teach me that loving God and abiding in Him are my primary aims in life. And in His kindness, He used this season of my heightened awareness of my dependence upon Him as the context in which He displayed His faithfulness to others through me.

LOVING GOD

In her chapter on singleness, Sydney reminded us of what the primary object of our love should be. We are to "love the Lord your God with all your heart, with all your soul, and with all your mind. This is the greatest and most important command. The second is like it: Love your neighbor as yourself" (Matt. 22:37–39). In saying this, Jesus indicts the religious leaders of falling short of keeping the law by neglecting this central task. All their piety and good works—bereft of love of God—add up to an exercise in missing the point. Missionaries are often susceptible to that same trap today.

A true disciple of Christ is to have one primary love. We are to love God more than anything else. Nothing else should take the throne of our hearts but Him. Now, it is easy to bring to mind self-centered things that might vie for the throne of our hearts. But this warning includes good things too. Neither ministry nor missions, neither leading a team nor shepherding our children, neither evangelism nor church work is to supplant our primary calling to love the Lord. We are to love Him above all else.

It is true that Jesus commands us to love our neighbor as ourselves in this passage, but neighbor love is to be derived first and foremost from our love of God. That means we cannot rightly love our neighbor if we do not keep God as our primary focus and love.

It is easy to *read* this in its proper order: first love God and then love neighbor. It is also easy to *write* it and verbally *affirm* it as fitting. But it can be hard to *live* it. The sense of urgency that arises from your love for the lost can cause your heart to face the sneaky temptation of putting the love of others on the throne of your heart in place of God.

To allow our labors among the lost to take priority over our walk with God is to disorder our lives and loves. Disordered loves result in disordered ministry. Such disorder will only harm our spiritual walk. Further, these disordered loves will tempt us to shift our dependence away from God and onto what we can do to save our neighbors in our own strength.

ABIDING IN HIM

So how do we maintain rightly ordered loves? Especially on the mission field—where we've given ourselves to the urgent task of serving the lost—how do we keep our hearts centrally focused on loving God?

I have personally found Jesus's Upper Room Discourse in John 15:1–8 to be a key to this balance. Here, in His last traumatic hours before the horrific events of His arrest and crucifixion, Jesus reminds His disciples of their need to remain attached to Him as a fruitful branch must remain connected to the life-giving vine. In verse 4, Jesus states: "Remain in me, and I in you. Just as a branch is unable to produce fruit by itself unless it remains on the vine, neither can you unless you remain in me." Another word that can be used for remaining is *abiding*. Apart from remaining or abiding in Christ, "you can do nothing" (v. 5).

Those words for a missionary hold both comfort and discomfort. We have no ability in our own power to produce fruit in our own lives or in others apart from remaining attached to the Vine. That is an uncomfortable reality, especially when we examine our hearts and realize how prone we are to relying on our own abilities and strength to accomplish things for God. However, this passage is also a source of comfort as Jesus instructs us to find our strength in our connection to the God who created all things and sustains them by His power. He is the source of our life, and He is the Life-Source who will save and redeem others through the fruit He bears in us.

At the risk of redundancy, then, let me just reiterate that the most essential part of the missionary life is maintaining your walk with the Lord. Abiding in Him is what will keep you moving forward when leaving all you love is hard. Abiding in Him is going to allow you to give grace in tense team situations. Abiding in Him is what will sustain you when singleness is hard, when marriage is hard, and when raising third-culture kids is hard. Abiding in Him is what is going to keep you walking to yet another language class and is what is going to propel you to keep sharing your faith in the middle of lots of rejection and, quite possibly, persecution. Abiding in Him is going to keep you steadfast when you face seasons of intense suffering that do not show signs of quickly letting up or getting easier. Abiding in Jesus should remain in your heart as your priority.

Before we move on to advice, however, I want to clear the air on one thing. I don't want you to hear by any means that missionary work is anything less than hard work, long hours, and intense effort. It should be this. You will be entering a job that has heavy responsibility. It is a process of walking with God, loving Him above all else, and declaring His goodness to people who need to hear it. It is nothing short of hard work. I don't want anything I am saying to nullify that. However, your love of God and persistence in abiding in Him must be the fuel for your work and ministry, lest it be labor without the Life-Source.

With that in mind, the following advice is born out of the reminders I kept before me each day and throughout each season. These reminders of the past gave me confidence for the future and strength in the present moments of daily grind, heart-wrenching rejection, and glorious conversion.

REMEMBER

Loving God and abiding in Him means recounting the miracle of your salvation.

Daily stand in awe of the gospel that has saved you. Especially if you grew up in a Christian home, it is easy to think your testimony is less that what it is. Your salvation story is an absolute miracle that God produced. Ephesians 2 reminds us that we were totally dead in our trespasses and sins (v. 1). Whether you believed when you were seven, thirty-seven, or seventy-seven, what was produced was by the power of the Spirit (vv. 4–9). Why am I reminding you of this? As you look around and look ahead at your days while you are overseas, the heaviness of the overwhelming task in front of you may feel like too much to bear. *You* can't do the job that is in front of you; it's impossible. However, remember that the same God who was perfectly in control of saving you is the same God who is in control of working the miracle of salvation in the people He is calling you to share with. The same miracle of salvation that has been done in your heart is the hope for the people you hold out the gospel to.

Loving God and abiding in Him means treasuring His Word and treasuring communion with Him.

Let your time with the Lord be what you look forward to in the morning and what you go to bed thinking about it. Psalm 1 speaks of one who delights in the law of the Lord and "meditates on it day and night" (v. 2). This person is described as being like a tree planted by flowing streams, who bears fruit in its season, does not wither, and whatever this person does prospers (v. 3).

Because of your love for Jesus and your remaining attached to Him, I pray, reader, that many would see this in you. I pray that your words would match your life because of the rightly ordered prioritization of your loves.

Loving God and abiding in Him means faithful obedience to the Great Commission.

You cannot save people any more than you were able to save yourself. But God, in His infinite wisdom, has chosen to use human messengers—fragile and cracked clay pots as we are—to be the vessels of His glorious salvation in Christ. Therefore, loving

God means obeying His command to "make disciples of all nations" (Matt. 28:19), even when we know we are powerless apart from Him to do so.

It's a funny thing to volunteer to pack up your belongings, quit your job, and move across the world to do something you are unable to do on your own. The average person would consider that slightly insane. However, as we prize knowing Jesus above all else, the burden of His love for the nations is easily transferable to our hearts. The Great Commission becomes a joy not because your church back home gives you super-Christian status because of your sacrifice, but because Jesus has been given "all authority" (Matt. 28:18) to carry out the Great Commission and He is "with you always, to the end of the age" (v. 20).

Loving God and abiding in Him means picking up your cross.

This may sound simplistic, but the life of a disciple should be patterned after Jesus. Now, I am not advocating looking for hardship or trials; however, most likely as you follow the Lord in obedience to the Great Commission, discipleship will at times look like picking up a cross. It will look like denial of what seems like should be due to you. It will look like following Jesus into places where the future seems unpredictable or uncertain. However, the beautiful irony of this call is found in Matthew 16:25. Somehow in the sovereignty of God, He orchestrates a finding of true life, while it appears to all others that His disciples are losing what should be most precious to them.

I remember staring at Facebook one day in our time overseas and watching as our peers back home bought their second or third homes. I watched as they took beautiful vacations and raised their babies close to grandparents. There is absolutely nothing wrong or sinful about these things; however, I knew that for that time, God had asked my family to do something different. My temptation was to focus on the easiness of what I perceived God's call on their lives to be, rather on the joy set before me in what obedience to Jesus looked like in my life. The missionary life does indeed look a lot like dying to preferences, ease of life, and comfort; however, the weight of the eternal value of what you are doing *is worth it.*

Loving God and abiding in Him is knowing with confidence that God wins.

The future is set and secure. Someplace in your home or maybe currently in your hands you have access to Revelation 21. We have a sure testimony of what is to come. God is coming to dwell with us (v. 3). You have heard testimony in this book to grief and hardship missionary life has brought. However, Jesus is coming back to wipe every tear from our eyes; death, grief, crying, and pain will be no more (v. 4). The nations may rage, but our King is on His throne (Ps. 2). He has given us a vision of what the end is, and He will bring it about. What that looks like is not a distant God who keeps His people at bay. Our future looks like God dwelling with us. He wins. We win because we get present and future life with Him.

I desperately want the good news of our Savior and King to be a reality known among the nations. And if you are reading this book, my guess is that is your heartbeat as well. Can you accomplish this desire? Absolutely not. However, until the day you draw your last breath, you can move forward to the places God takes you—worshiping, obeying, and loving Him with all your heart, soul, mind, and strength—and inviting others to do the same.

So, as you anticipate a move in the future or are possibly looking out at what is in front of you now, remember Paul's encouragement in 1 Corinthians 15:58 (ESV): "be steadfast, immovable, always abounding in the work of the Lord, knowing that in the Lord your labor is not in vain."

MY DEPENDANCE, HIS FAITHFULNESS

As I mentioned earlier, the season of life I was in during the beginning of 2016 was uniquely frustrating to my desires for productivity. I was especially aware of my limitations. But through this season I was also being taught how sweet it is to lean fully into my dependence upon the Lord.

He was doing a work teaching me that my self-reliance and pride I took in being a "hard worker" was less about glorifying Him and more about glorifying myself. He was producing in me the fruits of greater humility and dependence as I acknowledged my limitations and relied on Him in greater ways. I spent time both remembering and recounting His good works in the past and praised Him for what He could do in the future. Praise God that He continues His good work of sanctification and cares so deeply about holiness in our lives.

All the while He was doing this in me, He was answering my prayers to see my friends come to faith. During this season, the Lord kindly gave me the privilege of seeing one of the answers to my prayers in the life of a girl who, frankly, I had not expected to be a likely candidate for conversion.

Sometime during 2015, I had met a girl who I got along well with, but then I lost touch with her. We had hung out a few times and I had been able to share the gospel with her. However, she was much more interested in talking about coffee, hairstyles, and future marriage prospects than about spiritual things.

We lost contact for some time, so in 2016, I was surprised when, out of the blue, she texted me and asked if we could meet. I brought all three kids to the coffee shop, and when you show up with a three-year-old, a one-year-old, and a newborn, you end up being quite a show. I expected very little from that meeting outside of wanting to reconnect with an old friend. My friend came in the middle of my three-year-old attempting a headstand next to the table, and began by asking me about the Torah, Hinduism, Islam, and how I know for sure that Christianity is right. It was evident that God was working in her heart. He was creating a curiosity for eternal things.

God did an incredible work in my sweet friend's heart. It was not out of any eloquence of my words, or because of anything I could have brought about. In the year I spent on my knees, communing with the Father in a way I never had before, He was doing what only God can do. He was working in my friend to produce a curiosity and a desire to know God. All the while, God was doing an incredible work in my heart of allowing me to trust Him to do what only He can do. My priority was loving Him, abiding in Him, and out of that—obeying.

God brought about the miracle of salvation in my friend's heart. She read Scripture. She saw the depravity of her own heart, and she understood the goodness of God in providing a sacrifice for sin. God took her from death to life, and in His grace, He allowed me to read with her, reason with her, and pray with her, but watch Him do His work. I can say with honesty that one of the most incredible moments I have ever had was the day she told me that she believed. It was the day I got to watch her be symbolically buried with Christ in baptism and raised with Him to newness of life in Him.

The miracle God had done in me so many years ago, He now did in my friend. She now gets the incredible privilege of knowing Christ. She now gets to experience the peace that comes with remaining in Him. She now gets to be a part of sharing the gospel with her friends and family. She now gets the hope of knowing that, in the end, God wins.

CONCLUSION

This advice to cling to Jesus at all costs is not necessarily novel, and it is probably the same advice that each of the contributors to this book would give if asked for their number-one suggestion. All of us would agree that it is vital that you love the Lord your God with all your heart and put abiding in Him as your number-one priority.

I have heard of and met handfuls of people who are currently trying to go overseas and are doing everything right. They are in marriage counseling; they are seeking support from their church; they are seeking a team in which they can fit well; they are preparing their children for what may or could be ahead. However, when asked what their walk with the Lord looks like, they have answered, "Well, it is spotty, slightly inconsistent." At the risk of sounding legalistic, this answer terrifies me. It terrifies me that, at times, the calling to be a missionary can so quickly be given a higher priority than knowing and abiding in the One they hope to share.

Ladies, let this not be you. Love God above all else. Do the right things to prepare to go, work your tail off when you arrive and as you serve, but do not lose sight of the One who is the object of your worship. You cannot worship a calling, nor a place, nor a gospel-deprived people. Your worship is only due to God. He is the prize, the treasure in a field worth selling all you have in order to buy that field (Matt. 13:44). Don't forget that. Let your love for Him be your aim, and let your calling to a people or a place be born out of that love.

We are cheering you on. Cheering you on to an obedience born out of a love for God. Cheering you on, knowing that for each of you reading this, God has orchestrated your boundaries. He is all-sovereign and is working all of your comings and your goings out for His glory and His good purposes. We are praying for you, dear reader—*before you go.*

DISCUSS AND REFLECT

1. Recount the ways God has been good to you through the gospel. How did you hear it? Who shared it with you? Thank God for the ways He has been faithful to reveal Himself to you.

2. What do the daily rhythms of walking with God look like in your life right now? What are sins that you have been convicted of? What are ways you can see the Lord growing and changing you?

3. What can you foresee or see now as being difficulties of faithfully abiding in Christ on the field?

4. What are common temptations for you to prioritize over your relationship with God, both in your home country and outside?

5. How have you seen God work recently or in the past when you have prioritized prayer and seeking the Spirit's leading?

Contributors' Biographies

Cyndi Logsdon and her husband served with a missions organization for seventeen years, the majority of those years as church planters among an unreached people group in Central Asia. They led missionary teams in five countries and helped start a church in the city where they lived. During that season, Cyndi fell in love with sharing the gospel with Muslim women. They raised two daughters overseas and eventually moved back to the States to help lead training for future missionaries. Cyndi currently serves as the central director of church groups for McLean Bible Church in Vienna, Virginia. Cyndi is a pastor's wife who loves to teach the Bible, disciple new believers, and serve in the context of the local church.

Hilary Alan is the author of *Sent: How One Family Traded the American Dream for God's Greater Purpose.* She and her husband, Curt, served six years in Asia, and have been helping to encourage and develop missionaries and church planters all over the world since 2006. They have two grown children, and they currently serve in the Washington, DC, area.

C. J. Olivia grew up in North Carolina, but has lived internationally with her family for six years. She is married and has three young children. After graduating from the University of North Carolina at Chapel Hill in 2012, C. J. and her husband moved to North Africa, serving with the International Mission Board. In 2016, they joined Cafe 1040 to help mobilize the next generation of missionaries to the unreached peoples of the world. In 2019, C. J. and her family moved back overseas to start a new location for Cafe 1040's missions mentorship program. They work among North African and Middle Eastern people groups living in Europe, and are passionate about what God is doing among these people groups living in major European cities.

Lydia Pettus grew up in Virginia, but has spent the majority of her adult life working and living overseas to her heart's desire in some of the darkest unreached parts of the world. By God's plan and grace, she is joyfully single. After graduating from Virginia Commonwealth University in 1997, she left the United States for the very first time to work in Southeast Asia as an English teacher. The Lord has also led her to be a part of His work in Central Asia and Richmond, Virginia. She is deeply grateful to God for allowing her to be part of His work among the nations. Through the joys and the sorrows, she would not want to do anything else.

Ruth Ripken and her husband, Nik, are mission veterans of thirty-five years with the International Mission Board–SBC. They served in Malawi, South Africa, Kenya, Somalia, Germany, Ethiopia, and the Middle East. Ruth has a BA and master's in education from Georgetown College in Georgetown, Kentucky. They have done extensive research among believers living in the midst of persecution in more than seventy countries. Several books have been written to share the stories and lessons from these amazing believers. Nik is the author of *The Insanity of God: A True Story of Faith Resurrected* and *The Insanity of Obedience: Walking with Jesus in Tough Places.* In cooperation with B&H Publishing, a curriculum based upon both books was developed in 2016. A documentary based on *The Insanity of God* was released in 2016. In 2019, *The Insanity of Sacrifice*, a ninety-day devotional, was published.

Ruth and Nik spend their time now teaching in churches, schools, and with mission organizations as well as with believers around the globe. They currently minister through Nik Ripken Ministries.

Emily Watkins grew up in North Carolina and graduated from the University of North Carolina with a degree in nursing. She served in North Africa and the Middle East for seven years. Emily is married and has three children: Ella, Haley, and Ethan. Currently, she and her husband, Chris, are living in the Raleigh/ Durham area where she serves as the chief operations officer at Neighbor Health and her husband serves as director of sending at The Summit Church.

Sydney Dixon is currently serving in South Asia with the International Mission Board. She was formerly a staff member of Cru (previously called Campus Crusade for Christ), serving in both Russia and Eastern Europe, and on the national leadership team. She has an MDiv from Southeastern Baptist Theological Seminary in counseling. She is currently finishing her PhD in international church planting.

Amy Bowman was born and raised in Jacksonville, Florida, but lived internationally for seventeen years with her family. She is the wife of Joshua and mother to four children. She graduated with a BSN from Jacksonville University and married the love of her life. In 2002, Amy and Joshua, along with their firstborn, moved to Africa to serve with the International Mission Board as church planters in a rural village in Northern Zambia. Three children later in 2010, Amy and her family transitioned to one of the most densely populated cities in South Asia, where they served until 2019. Amy currently lives with her family in Cedarville, Ohio, where her husband is a professor at Cedarville University. Amy is hopeful she might return to teaching women under a mango tree someday, but for now she loves mentoring the next generation of women who are called to the unreached.

Nina Buser and her husband, Brooks, met at San Diego Christian College and were married after she graduated with a degree in counseling psychology. During her years at college, she heard about missions among unreached language groups. Through that initial exposure, and a steady diet of good teaching from their local church, Nina and Brooks decided they would go and give their lives to plant a church among those who have never heard the gospel and have no church among them. After two years of training in 2003 they, along with their three-year-old son, left for the country of Papua New Guinea and eventually moved in among the YembiYembi people. By God's grace, they were able to become fluent in the language of the YembiYembi, develop an alphabet, teach the YembiYembi how to read and write, translate the Scriptures, and see the YembiYembi church born and brought to maturity. Thirteen years later, that church now has its own elders, deacons, and the translated Word in their language. Nina and Brooks now serve with Radius International, training up the next generation to go plant churches among unreached language groups.

Emily Bennett grew up in Clinton, Wisconsin. She attended Winona State University and completed her bachelor's in education. She met her husband, Matt, in college, and they worked on staff with InterVarsity Christian Fellowship for two years together. It was through the ministry of InterVarsity and the Urbana Missions Conference that both Emily and Matt felt a growing desire to be trained and sent as missionaries. Before moving overseas, she completed a master of divinity and a master of arts in intercultural studies from Southeastern Baptist Theological Seminary. Emily and Matt served in North Africa for seven years with their three children: Anabelle, Elliot, and Oliver. They are currently living in Ohio, working with an organization that helps internationals learn English and transition to life in the United States. Matt is a professor at Cedarville University, and they love encouraging future missionaries both from the university as well as in their local church.

Notes

1. *Foundations*, International Mission Board, 65.

2. *Foundations*, International Mission Board, 65.

3. David Platt, *Mission Precision* (David Platt and Radical Inc., 2018).

4. R. C. Sproul, *Everyone's a Theologian: An Introduction to Systematic Theology* (Sanford, FL: Reformation Trust Publishing, 2014).

5. John Piper, "May I Help You Discern Your Calling?," Desiring God, https://www.desiringgod.org/articles/may-i-help-you-discern-your-calling. Accessed January 10, 2023.

6. Amy Carmichael, *Candles in the Dark* (Fort Washington, PA: CLC Publications, 1981), 28.

7. John Piper, "What Does It Mean to Be Made in God's Image?" https://www.desiringgod.org/interviews/what-does-it-mean-to-be-made-in-gods-image.

8. In 2018 the ERLC compiled information reporting that one in three women view porn on a weekly basis and 56 percent of women twenty-five and younger actively seek out porn. Mikayla Simpson, "What You Should Know about Women and Pornography," *The Ethics & Religious Liberty Commission,*

September 20, 2018, https://erlc.com/resource-library/articles/what-you-should-know-about-women-and-pornography/.

9. Elisabeth Elliot, *A Chance to Die: The Life and Legacy of Amy Carmichael* (Ada, MI: Revel, 1987).